The Care & Feeding of Southern Men

*A Survival Guide
for the
Unsuspecting
Yankee*

The Care
& Feeding of
Southern
Men

*A Survival Guide
for the Unsuspecting Yankee*

BY CLAUDIA GRECO

ILLUSTRATED BY CHRIS OBRION

Algonquin Books of Chapel Hill   *1987*

Published by
Algonquin Books of Chapel Hill
Post Office Box 2225
Chapel Hill, North Carolina 27515-2225

in association with
Taylor Publishing Company
1550 West Mockingbird Lane
Dallas, Texas 75235

Illustrations © copyright 1987 by Chris OBrion.
Design by Molly Renda.

Library of Congress Cataloging-in-Publication Data
Greco, Claudia, 1960–
Care and feeding of southern men.

1. Men—Southern States—Anecdotes, facetiæ,
satire, etc. 2. Southern States—Social life and customs—Anecdotes, facetiæ, satire, etc. I. Title.
HQ1090.5.A13G74 1987   305.3'1'0975   86-28676
ISBN 0-912697-60-1

To the two Gladyses,
Big and Little
and, of course, to Ed—
with whom it all began

Author's Note

This book is written, for the most part,
in English and Virginian (Southern
Highland and Southern Coastal Dia-
lects), as opposed to a Deep South dia-
lect, due to the mixed origins of the
people involved. Readers from the Gulf
Coast, Arkansas, and most of Texas
should therefore approach some of the
dialogue with extreme caution.

Contents

Preface

For the record, it was all his fault.

It was either stay with him, leave him, or write a book.

I wrote. It was cheaper than therapy.

Don't get me wrong; he was a fun guy—under certain conditions. These were when he was:

    (a) sober

    (b) conscious

    (c) not in a Southern mood

The third was a little tricky, considering he was a Southerner. Usually he could manage (b) if he wasn't (a), but (c) almost always required drastic action. Getting all these operatives into place at the same time, however, demanded the strategic cunning of a ninja assassin.

He was a ninja. He arose, in darkness, on occasion, crawling through the underbelly of the night, and you'd never know where or when he'd strike. I'd get abrupt phone calls from uptown, midtown, downtown; from boats he hid out on and bars he haunted; from the McDonald's he threatened to trash and the victims he *had* trashed, and sometimes he'd just suddenly appear, slicing his way through the black, at my doorstep. Grinning and licking the blood off his teeth.

Mayhem was a compulsion with him. He swore his fights were a matter of avenging Southern honor; I know they were more an outgrowth of the Southern Macho Male Mystique. Yankees may be partly responsible for propagating the image of Dixie men as brawling, drawling, chitlin-bred anarchists, but I know at least one Good Ol' Bawh who did his level best to make sure that notion died hard. In one case, I concede he was within his rights to beat a particular antagonist into Alpo; but if the truth be told—and it shall—I suspect he was really responding to a secret, joyous tribal call, an evil and primordial glee in chaos, crisis, and putting his womenfolks' blood pressure up.

There were more weird and wonderful—and frequently unfathomable—regional traits of his that I was to discover as time went by, and the more I thought about it, the more it occurred to me that someone, somewhere, should have drafted some guidelines to help the average Northern woman sidestep the yawning cultural gap before her. Little things like ... well ... language, for instance; her new ranking in the Grits Oligarchy (somewhat behind the Dawg and a little ahead of fishing); and, most importantly, Surviving The Southern Male.

So I wrote. I could smell the sudden fear on him as he realized—too late!—what I'd known for years: that writing well is the best revenge, even if you aren't out for blood. I was concerned that I might appear malicious. His concern was more basic.

"She wouldn't really go through with this, would she?" he asked my brother. He grinned his best alligator grin—lopsided. Disarming. Mischievous. *Nervous*. The sickening truth had just hit him—*he* had suggested the book.

Beloved sibling pondered the other man's question momentarily. "Yep," he answered, "I believe she would."

"She cay-yan't!" protested my Southern Male, "Ah'm her honey!"

Chris smiled at him malevolently. "You," he retorted, "are her *material*." And he was. Or, more accurately, became so.

Because every now and then, when the maniacal gleam in his eye softened, he'd set his beer down and stop adoring the Dawg long enough to inform me, via syrupy drawl, that I sure enough was his su-gah of deep affection—even if I was a Yankee. And it made learning—and surviving—the rules all worth it.

Maybe.

New York
May, 1985—November, 1986

The Care
& Feeding of
Southern
Men

A Survival Guide
for the
Unsuspecting
Yankee

i. Rednecks

1 *The Random Rules of Survival*

(1) Know Your Rednecks.

It is essential that you be able to spot a Southern Man before he spots you. That way, you can avoid little conversational misunderstandings about the superiority of Yankee schools, Yankee food, or Yankee civilization. Or just Yankees in general.

As the South catches up in affluence, education and options, it has become harder to be able to tell some Southerners from their Northern counterparts; Southern Yuppies, after all, aspire to a lot of the things that non-Southern Yups do, so some assimilation is inevitable. But keeping in mind that Suppies were once Rednecks or at least Good Ol' Bawhs, a few guidelines for spotting them still hold true. A Good Ol' Bawh is anyone born with:

      (a) a wrench
      (b) a fishing pole, or
      (c) a can of beer in his hand.

A Good Ol' Bawh is also anyone answering to:

      (a) "Bubba"
      (b) "Goobuh"
      (c) any two first names
      (d) . . . preferably followed by "Lee."

And they are still allergic to consonants.

Knowing your Rednecks is vital in a room crowded full of strange men, so you then know to:

(2) Nevvuh Hum The Theme From "Deliverance" Out Loud.

This knowledge may save your life. Whether your Southern Man
is a lawyer from the southwest side of D.C., or a chicken farmer
from Sludge Gully, Alabama, he will still take immediate and vi-
olent umbrage at the implied insult. Good Ol' Bawhs are usually
large, gregarious, flamboyant guys; Rednecks, rangy, taciturn
brooders whose lips never move. Both groups move pretty well,
however, upon hearing the first bar or so of "Dueling Banjos," so
the best thing you can do, should some naive fellow-Yankee com-
mit this indiscretion, is to deny ever having seen the movie, and
ask—loudly—who gives diddly-squat about an aging, balding,

fattening Hollywood cracker called Burt Somebody, *anyway*?! ("Piss-ant!") Another pitfall to avoid is:

(3) Nevvuh Feed Quiche To A Redneck.

This alarms and confuses them. Sure, you can get quiche in McLean, Virginia, or in Richmond or in various sissy cities in the Tidewater, but even the most urbane Southern Male will regard it with the deepest suspicion. Taking him Up North, out of his natural habitat, won't help; he'll just crash around Manhattan or Chicago or wherever, cursing Yankee cuisine and mourning the dearth of Real Food. Southern Men don't ever convert—they convert you, so just remember:

(4) Into Each Life, Some Grits Must Fall—

(5) Even In New York.

It is therefore in your best interests to know where to be able to lay ahold of Real Grits, fish roe, and other Dixie delicacies at any hour of the day or night. That way, when your poah' honey comes in after a hard night/morning/weekend of looking for the Ultimate Brew in this gawd-fo'saken Yankee city you make him live in, you can at least placate him with the grits an' aigs an' hay-yum (*country* ham—not that gawddamn pink plastic Yankee garbage!). Because you know as well as he does that there ain't no real beer, bourbon, or booze of no kahhnd *in* Yankeeland, to begin with.

Other lifesaving ploys include not only not interfering with Drinkin' Nahhht (re: "pursuit of happiness,") but also the free exercise of his religion (guaranteed under the Constitution). This entails, among other things, that you:

(6) Always Be Stoic During Football.

This goes beyond mere Religion, into the realm of primeval Tribal Rites. His Celtic ancestors used to sacrifice young men to the Druidic gods in the Irish bogs and the plains of southern England; after five thousand years, it should at least be reassuring that he is consistent in preserving family tradition. It also makes Footbawhl a lot more appealing.

The most critical element of this ritual is also the one most misunderstood by both Yankees and women. Yankee Women, therefore, must be doubly careful to avoid a common and fatal *faux pas* they aren't even aware of. Remember, he promised to love, honor, cherish, and keep you—but not everywhere. So, however much you come to resent their symbiosis,

(7) Nevvuh Come Between A May-yan And His Hound Dawg.

Every Southern Man is born with a Hound Dawg, which is placed in his crib at the moment of birth. These are always large, robust, and amiable canines of dubious origins, who cheerfully do everything except what you tell them to do—or nothing at all. It is not mandatory that a Hound Dawg be of bloodhound, basset hound, or other Hound Dawg extraction—in fact, the more mysterious its genetic mix, the better—but the Dawg can nevvuh be purebred. Or small. Small yappy dogs are *not* Dawgs; they are for sissies and old Yankee women and are therefore Out. Hound Dawgs are big, dumb, malodorous people necessitating the use of a forklift to hoist them whenever they feel inclined to collapse on Dai-dy's Yankee girlfriends' laps. Which is frequently. This, in turn, leads to:

(8) Nevvuh EVVUH Feed A Hungry Hound Dawg.

Hound Dawgs only get hungry when you're in the house, alone, with your overdue tax paperwork spread out on the living room floor, or while you're trying to flea-dip a hysterical cat; in which case, Dawgs will then volunteer their help. Don't, however, ever suspect that they appreciate your care of them: at best, they'll just eat, belch, amble off and wait, pining, for Dai-dy to come home; at worst, they won't. Which means that the Dawg will then roll over onto whatever you're working on, and demonstrate a certain sleepy, gaseous gratitude . . . again, only till Dai-dy gets back. Then It will ignore you. ("It," in this instance, meaning the Dawg.) Fortunately, Hound Dawgs go just about everywhere Dai-dy goes, so you don't really need to fully:

(9) Understand Redneck Day-Care.

This is your mate's long suit, and comes under Bringing Up Bird Dawg.

Now that you think you have your place in the Chitlin Mafia established, think again. Southern Men have a slew of subtle and bewildering priorities both within and outside of The Family, and it will take the better part of a Yankee Female's lifetime to identify and determine the importance of each. One easy way out is to just

(10) Don't Nevvuh Forget That Everything Is "His."

Such as:
- (a) *His* Mama
- (b) *His* Hound Dawg
- (c) *His* Family, and
- (d) *His* Woman.

Ranking them correctly, however, is Your Problem.

Certain things always stay in their designated places (namely, Woman), but depending on the time of the year, you may find your Southern Male undergoing a raging, all-consuming spiritual metamorphosis. You may find that His Mama, as important as she is, has just been displaced by that solemn religious period known as Footbawhl Season; she may even, occasionally, get bumped by His Dawg. Other seasonal considerations are, of course, His Foah'-Bah-Foah', His Gun, His Fishin' Tackle, and, always, His Turf.

(11) Make Sure You Know What A Foah'-Bah-Foah' Is.

First of all, be aware that this vehicle has different names. In Virginia, West Virginia, and the Carolinas, it's called a Foah'-Bah-Foah'; in South Carolina, Georgia, Alabama, and Florida, however, it's a Fo'-Bah-Fo'; and anywhere north of Kentucky, you might know it as a four-by-four. Its basic function all over the South is, nonetheless, the same: to cram into it as many Good Ol' Bawhs, Hound Dawgs, crates of moonshine and stray females as are humanly possible. No other pick-up truck has ever been put to so imaginative a use.

Once you get really good at surviving the relationship, you can then begin to enjoy your Southern Man—it's not all hard work and neurosis. But far more important than understanding his heritage, far more significant than believing in his mythology, is mastering a phase of adjustment absolutely crucial to you both; this is called making an effort to:

(12) Learn The Language.

Not every woman will experience speaking in tongues in her life-time, but you will. Your eyes will glaze over, your head will jerk spasmodically, and before you can wipe the froth from your foaming lips, you will lose any previous ability you possessed to communicate in English . . . or anything remotely like it. Sometimes this happens slowly, after hours of dawg-eared dipthongs and lop-sahhded vowels further complicated by tortuous grammatical configurations; but sometahhms, awhhl it tay-yeks is one little ol' Christian wuhhd lahhk "hellacious," or "instructifah-yin'," or "piss-ant," to set you awhhff. Understanding your soulmate through a Southern accent isn't all that hard; understanding him through the unique use of Dixie words and grammar is. Be warned, therefore: bah th'tahhm you unduh-stan' him, it'll be too late for *you*.

2 *The Meeting of the Twain*

Sometime in 1983, I converted.
I don't mean an old-time-Holy-Jesus-revival-camp conversion—hell, no; I mean a Conversion.

Let me put that in its proper context. I had a father who believed life stopped west of the Hudson and south of Staten Island, and a mother whose sum knowledge of grits barely made it beyond a John Wayne movie and ground-in dirt. I myself was born, lived, and worked in New York; the fact that I spoke accentless, well-enunciated English was never held against me. But in 1983, something went very wrong.

I started going out with the Southerner.

Hence my remarks about Conversion. As I said before, you never convert a Son of the South—he converts you. The first thing that goes, of course, is the syntax. Grammatical structure begins, like multi-headed hydra, to take on a life of its own; then slowly, stealthily—but irrevocably—with the dreaded finality of a congenital disease, the enunciation deteriorates . . . the creeping metastasis of fuzzy phonemes . . . this is where the letter "i" ceases to exist except in print, and what is left to be understood as English gets mauled further by Dixian aphorisms and other idiomatic perversions.

This is why so many Yankees sound Southern. Ignoring, for

the moment, the Conversion element and the frenzy for Cuisine du Sud currently raging through the States, there are numerous reasons why even a Yuppie from Cos Cob would trash sixteen years' worth of The Right Schools and a large chunk of Mommy's trust fund to sound Southern—and they don't have diddly-squat to do with Nouvelle Fatback.

There is, of course, the Rakish Macho/Virility Factor. Good Ol' Bawhs have a reputation for being ba-a-add-to-the-bone, freewheeling hedonists—but always with flair. Look at Rhett Butler. Look at Edwin Edwards. Lots of ladies have a weird electric affinity for ba-a-add, dashing, dangerous men, and Northern men are finally getting hip to it.

The second reason, naturally, is also the Macho/Virility Factor.

Dixie Men like Footbawhl just three ways: loud, bloody, and lots of it—preferably live, but via TV or radio will do nicely, too. Without any statistics available, I would guess that maybe half to two-thirds of the professional Conferences are composed of Southern-born or -trained players, and whoever isn't, secretly wishes he was. Look at Joe Namath; who the hell remembers he was born in Beaver Falls, Pennsylvania, when he and every other closet Southerner have been drawling at the nation over the air all these years?

And the third reason, yet again, is likewise the Macho/Virility Factor. Drawls are in, and this I blame on Chuck Yeager as much as Joe Namath. Yeager was once so cornpone to the marrow that his own wife could just about understand him; but he was a *May-yan*, bah Gawd!, a Living Legend even before he broke the sound barrier—which was about the only thing that the military fly-boys and the civilian pilots (most of whom had military training) ever respected. So that sawhhft, easy-goin', hidy-holler ol' Drawhhl got carried on the channels of the radios crackling high above Edwards Air Force Base, to Houston, where Yeager taught aeronautics to future astronauts, and to damn near every fighter jock-turned-commercial pilot who ever eased a plane down a foot of runway. The military aviators who moved into the Mercury space program naturally became bona fide Heroes in their own right, although the Original Seven were not Yeager protegés—nor, necessarily, were they Southern-born. But a few of them came across like it—"Gordo" Cooper, for instance, a native Oklahoman, and two Midwesterners who became known to the world as "Gus" and "Deke." And then someone had to go and release the movie, *The Right Stuff.* In an election year. With the first American to orbit the earth running for president.

The fourth reason, of course, is Conversion.

You would suppose, with the emergence of New South Preppies/Yuppies, that there would be a lot less Conversion taking place. You would also be wrong.

It pretty much depends on what a Suppie wears.

In Sassons and a polo shirt, my Southern-born beloved was cosmopolitan Richmondese—Southern, to be sure, but from a border state—the Shallow South. In a Saint-Laurent shirt and parachute pants he was essentially a transplanted New Yorker who may have been either dyslexic or bilingual (depending on your viewpoint); but in Levis—lawhhng, sawhhn-awhff, new-blue, or faded—he was a Suth-nuh. Forget about the shirt.

I went out with him for nearly a year before I ever saw him out of Lee-vahs. The rot had already set in by then. Richmond, Virginia, isn't that far south (unless you happen to come from there), but there is no one more Southern—regardless of native city—than a Southern boy besieged by a horde of argyle-clad, Perrier-guzzling Yankees. Most Northerners think that the drawhl thickens up the farther south you go, just because that's what they hear all around them; the truth of it is, the farther *north* you transplant a Southerner, the more down-home he becomes.

So the voice—and through it, the soul—of Dixie is really quite safe from the onslaught of Yankee assimilation . . . just as long as there's blue denim, Footbawhl, and aggravating elitist Yankees to fuel it.

Yankee culture, however, may never be the same again.

3 *Caveat Emptor, Honey Chile*

I must admit, my mother took the news about my choice of boyfriend fairly well.

"Southern?!" Her head came up with a jerk as she skewered me with a baleful eye. "How far south?"

There was a certain logic to her question. Her mother was raised in Louisiana, and both parents live in Texas, but she still had a Yankee mother's conception of Dixie men.

My father was somewhat blunter. "Is he inbred?" he inquired, all sweetness. "No!" I snapped, "He's a *Virginian!*" Oh.

I didn't dispute the fact that Southern men have an image problem. They aren't all as suave as Rhett Butler, but they also aren't as rustic as the Dukes Of Hazzard, or as rabidly depraved as the *Deliverance* hillsmen (although they do have their moments). Hence my parents' touching concern.

"Well," sighed my Daddy, "then he might learn to read, yet . . . "

It was His Mama, not mine, who shed some light on the image/conflict issue. We were out in the suburban/rural fringes of Richmond in search of barbecue, when she suddenly decided to pull into this tiny neighborhood eatery. It was a nice enough place; mostly wood from ceiling to floor, a few dusty bulbs to light the stark walls, paint peeling like a skin disease . . . it smelled "real" to me.

It was.

"Look!" chirped His Mama, pointing to the bar, "Rednecks!"

I blinked incredulously. Here was a woman whose entire clan lived thirty-five miles from the nearest city, in a hamlet whose residents freely admit is a cow town, and she stood marveling at the local yokels. I was obviously missing a critical distinction, one I'm still not sure exists.

"They're Rednecks," she explained, throwing an arm each around her husband and younger son, "*mah* men are Good Ol' Bawhs."

I weighed the information carefully. Several seconds passed before I could bring myself to talk.

"Uhh-huhhh," I hedged. "What's the difference?"

His Mama impaled me on a steely glare. Truly, I had devolved into some unspeakable creature, some unmentionable . . . organism devoid of any redeeming qualities . . . some . . . *tacky* . . . lesser life-form like a . . . a . . . *Yankee*! She drew herself up to her full five feet. "The difference," she seethed, "is *Breeding*."

Not income or education, mind you, but Breeding. Every society has lines of demarcation drawn across between its classes, but Down South, I found, the lines blur somewhat. Southern Men are the only men in the world who boast of their direct descension from the ancient kings of Ireland and then tell you, in the same breath, how they came up from mill-hand, dirt-farming or cotton-picking stock in a single generation. Sure, their whole tribe may still be running the ridges or living among the sunken stumps of Hell Hole Swamp, but ain't it also true that Cousin Jimmy Ray Cobbs is the mayor of Beulahville—and didn't Uncle Issum Scraggs land himself a congressional seat a tahhm back, oh, in 19-an'-55? That makes your Southern Man, by extension, a Su'nn Gennelmun; but hey, sure, he's still a regular Good Ol' Bawh. Visits Dai'dy's step-Mama's half-brother's in-laws in the bogs once, twice a year, don't he?

Southern Men, I decided, must come in four or five distinct types:

      (1) Fus' Famlya-vah-ginn-yuh (not Nawh-Carolahna or Looz-yanna, who, as any true Virginian knows, are merely plebian upstarts)
      (2) Suth-unn Gennelmun
      (3) Good Ol' Bawhs
      (4) Rednecks
      (5) Trash

First Families, obviously, are rife with Suth-unn Gennelmun, although such men can crop up elsewhere—and, thankfully, do. Southern Preppies (who *do* enunciate the "th"), can also be from a First Family, although their parents may well have been Good Ol' Bawhs—they're really New South Yuppies (Suppies). Good Ol' Bawhs are just that: regular, down-to-earth guys who are highly susceptible to drinking, fishing, Footbawhl, pretty women, and Hound Dawgs (not necessarily in that order). And Trash? Well, honey, if you have to ask, you don't have no kahhnd of class. . . .

But what differentiates a Redneck from a Good Ol' Bawh?

His Dai-dy grinned hugely. "Y'all see that wad'a chewin' tobaccah that bawh's gawhht?"

"Yeah," I told him. "That's it? Tobacco or no tobacco?"

He shook his head, gestured at the bare, sticky floor, and grinned even wider. "Y'all happen t'see a spitoon?"

Oh, no, not *that*, surely—

Dai-dy was positively beaming now. "Chile, there's but one thing separating us from them, especially in a sem-mah rural county." He edged forward in his chair, swelling with conspiratorial anticipation. "Good Ol' Bawhs raise lahhvstawhhk," he confided, "Rednecks get emotionally invawwhlved with *theirs*."

Raucous laughter. The Good Ol' Bawh contingent was getting a lot of mileage out of this, no question. The Rednecks continued to nurse their beers moodily. I was obviously getting nowhere fast, when His Dai-dy leaned forward one more time.

"Seriously, there is one clear lahhn of separation," he admitted.

"Like what," I retorted, "polyester?"

He squinted quickly at his trousers and scowled. "No . . . it's Attitude."

Hmmmmm. Attitude. Not much to go on. But it occurred to me, studying the other group around the bar, that Dai-dy just might be right. It wasn't so much a question of socio-economics as it was Mentality. . . .

HOW TO SPOT A REDNECK

(1) Look At The Clothes.

There are certain essential elements of attire that no self-respecting Redneck would be caught dead without. These are:

      (a) a plaid workshirt (with or without a T-shirt underneath)

      (b) battered denims

      (c) big workboots

      (d) a large brass belt buckle (preferably with the name of a brew on it)

      (e) a "Gimme!" cap

      (f) the beer (in hand)

(2) Elements Of Conversation.

      (a) farm machinery

      (b) cars

      (c) trucks

      (d) fishing

      (e) drinking

      (f) hound dawgs

(3) Religion.

      (a) footbawhl

(4) Food.

      (a) anything involving Hawg

      (b) beer

Rednecks, I discovered, were somewhat limited in their scope, but at least they were good sports about their public image. They take a kind of perverse/inverse pride in their Redneckhood, about coming from wild, rugged, highly individualistic stock, about their fierce, flinty Celtic rectitude honed by generations of hardship. . . . But it's a lot like coming from East New York, the South Side of Chicago, or East Los Angeles; an out-sider shouldn't make Too Much Of It—not if he/she cares to be ambulatory tomorrow. This, coupled with a brooding, Brando-esque ferocity, a certain reticence and what I can only describe as The Look, has catapulted Redneckhood into the realm of Mystique. It's Tough. It's Strong. And it's Ba-a-ad. It also has everything to do with Mind-Set.

We were headed into midtown Manhattan, my Southern Male and I, after a long day on the boat. He wanted to eat at his favorite place—a place where they knew and adored him, but where they kept the entire clientele waiting forever just to let them know who was boss. That night, however, was to be different.

"Ah'm goin' Redneck," he hissed. His eyes glinted evilly. I flinched. The metamorphosis was frightening. Fraying Lee-vahs, track shoes, and a T-shirt of dubious origin . . . a sleeveless khaki flak vest, complete with stenciling . . . the mandatory baseball cap . . . a toothpick (Oh, God, I forgot about the tooth-pick—he didn't have any chewing tobacco), and . . . The Look: his eyes sunk into black, granite cracks, the eyebrows furrowed dangerously, and the toothpick jutting pugnaciously from his bared teeth. . . .

And it worked. Busboys dropped dishes, waiters fled, and even the maitre d' turned pale as he stomped in, smirking crook-edly and hooking his thumbs through his belt-loops.

"Ah'd lahhk table foah'," he murmured, his voice ever so gentle.

The maitre d' winced. "I'm sorry, table four is reserved . . . uh . . . sir." My erstwhile Redneck reflected on that for about a second. Then, without a word, he snatched the "RESERVED" card off the damask, and handed it to a fishing buddy. *He* ate it.

"Just t'educate th'waiter," he explained, smiling seraphically.

The seating was done in a rapid blur.

We went back a few nights later. He was wearing a silk Cardin shirt and parachute pants this time, and while everyone was gracious and gregarious, we waited. And waited. Finally, he peeled open a tote bag he'd brought along, rummaged through it, and pulled out the flak vest, toothpick, shades and a "Gimme!" cap. Once again, the effect was electric. Waiters scuttled like cock-roaches, the manager bowed and scraped, and even the maitre d' began dropping strawberries into our Perignon. . . .

It wasn't until dessert that he found the heart to let the res-taurant staff off the hook. As the waiter advanced on him with the check, he snapped down his platinum AmEx card, pulled off his disguise, and spat out the toothpick.

"Hey, y'all!" he boomed, all dimples and innocence.

The maitre d's face cracked into fragments as he soundlessly dematerialized. The entire episode, it was clear, had been altogether too much for him. The waiters merely looked uncomfortable.

Later, as we sat down to our fourth gratis bottle of champagne with the now-sheepish owner, my Good Ol' Bawh commented on life's little ironies with wry satisfaction.

"Funny what a little thing lahhk clothes can do," he mused.

Recalling his gimlet eyes, shot red and raw and as ferocious as a rabid Doberman's, and the defiant toothpick clenched between his teeth, I smiled into my drink and pulled his baseball cap over his face.

"Wrong, sportsfan," I told him, "it's Attitude."

Then stuck his toothpick back in his teeth.

ii. Language

4 *Que Pasa, Y'all?*

To this day, I'm not sure how we managed to communicate. Either he picked up enough English over the years (yes, even in New York), or I had unknowingly developed the gift of speaking in tongues; at any rate, we got by. For the most part.

The least part was when both of us assumed the other spoke the Queen's English; both of us, therefore, were somewhat mystified by the seeming torrent of linguistic abuse we each used to reply to the other. In his case, the introduction of a new noun was enough to alarm him. What did it for me, though, was the effortless ability with which he—and all of his fellow Confederates—created adjectives and adverbs where none had previously existed.

Take white-water rafting. We were debating the merits of various Southern waterways, and he was trying to convince me that the only way to really experience such a trip was to do the rapids in the water. On a log.

"You've got to be kidding," I told him. "Don't you know how bad the rocks and the currents in the James are?"

His eyebrows skyrocketed. "Th'Jay-yems!" he exclaimed, "Hell, thass jus' a small little Christian rivvuh!"

I felt a synapse short-circuit. Visions of denominational rivers sprang up in my head: Hasidic rivers of flowing black . . . Catholic ones with a million little offshoots . . . Protestant ones with all the right entrées to the next tributary, or—no, that analogy was too much, even for me. I shook my thoughts back into place.

"Christian?" I queried.

"Yeah," he insisted, just a tad defensive, "You *know* . . . "

I concentrated furiously. "Like . . . meek? Humble? Unassuming? *Tame?*"

He beamed. "Yeah!" He pushed up his shades and politely bared his teeth. "Ah jus' knew you'd learn t'tawhhk rahht!"

I gritted my teeth to splinters. "*Right*?!" I hissed. "You couldn't tell a split infinitive from a hole in the ground, and you're giving me 'right'?!!"

"Sure," my mate informed me. "Th' wuhhd works, d'un'nit?"

Yes, I could see how it just might. That, I ascertained, was the cornerstone of Southern speech: if the word "works"—if it is descriptive, imaginative and powerful, it's right. And if it's right, you keep it. And then you improve on it.

I had to respect the Southerners' spoken words. Not so much for the soft, rolling slowness with which they're delivered in most corners of Dixie, nor even for the various accents, but rather, for their aptness. There's an incisiveness to them born of isolation, of insularity from the forward push of the rest of the world; but if the Dixie tongue is a half-step behind modern English, it is light years ahead in color.

Take insults. A Yankee might call an antagonist any number of names, but they'll all be nouns. A Southerner will wield not only the perfect noun, but also several choice and pungent adjectives to go with it. Hand-waving, volume, and rhetoric may do just fine for the rest of the nation, but Down South, it's specifics that count.

I recall one memorable occasion when my Old Dominion–born beloved locked horns with a native New Jerseyite. I listened in morbid fascination as his bourbon-smooth vowels got gored by the metallic consonants of the Northerner but it was the Good Ol' Bawh who got the final word:

"Yeah, Ah mahht very well be a SOB," he snarled, "but you . . . are a . . . no-'count . . . *lo-o-oo-oww* lahhff . . . sorry-ass . . . PISS-ANT!" The New Jerseyite's face collapsed, his eyes pinwheeling in shock. Clearly, he had been prepared for any one of a number of epithets, but not this. This encompassed heritage, genes, upbringing, and intelligence in one breath.

"A . . . a *what*?!" he stammered, weakly.

The Southerner ripped his eyes off his adversary and slowly shook his head. "Yeah, Ah reckon you sho' nuff are a pissant," he muttered, "'cause you sho' as hell are the sorriest-lookin' excuse for a may-yan *Ah* evvuh seen!"

Oh.

We had many other such moments. Out on the open sea, miles from land, I was trying to determine our approximate distance from Sayville.

"How far out are we, love?" I asked my Southern Male.

He squinted out over the water, absently nibbling his cigarette butt. "Ohhh," he mused, "a fawh' piece, Ah reckon."

"Fur piece"? Like . . . a stole? Ermine tails? Truly, this was a new nautical term for me. I mentally ran down every word in our common vocabulary, searching frantically for anything that might link animal pelts with life on the high seas.

"Ummmmm . . . could you be a little more specific?"

His eyes shot sparks. "Fawh' is fawh'," he spat. "If Ah knew how fawh' we were, Ah'd tell you!"

I looked out uncertainly across the wide expanse of ocean. The realization suddenly hit home—we were out a far piece, all right.

"Okay, Ahab," I told our intrepid captain, "we've got a slip held, in any case, so we don't have to kill ourselves getting there—unless, of course, you'd care to eat before nightfall."

"Nuh-uhhh," he said, "dinnuh or no dinnuh, we gawhht t'get alawwhng smart-quick." He pointed to the darkening, evil-looking horizon. "Looks lahhk it's comin' up a cloud." I allowed he had a point there, but I was never sure about his final observation:

"Mmmmmm-HMMMMMMM," he breathed, all heart-felt earnest, "this ill weathuh's followin' us around lahhk some haint done up ahn' put th'mouth awhhn us!"

Uhhhhhhh . . . right . . .

The problem got worse the farther south we went. The accents of all Southerners thicken up whenever one of them goes home with Yankees in tow, mainly for the benefit of those aforementioned Yankees (who, being tacky folk, eat that cornpone stuff up every time). He, however, went one better; he regressed so strongly into South Carolinian, that even his own Virginia-bred clan had trouble understanding him (a few years in a foreign country will do that to you, I guess). It just further convinced me that Southerners, as a people, created their various subdialects for the express purpose of confusing the non-Southerners. Insularity had nothing to do with it.

Take the word "with." In Virginia, it can be "with," "wi'," or even "wif," depending, but the deeper south you go, the more nebulous the word becomes. He and I had just got back from

Jackson County, North Carolina, and he was doing his best to persuade me to head off to Brandeville for an event whose purpose I never fully determined.

"Gawddahhm, girl," he burst out, "they jus' havin' th'bigges' t'row-down in Vah-ginn-yuh ovvuh theah!"

I eyed him cautiously. He and I had terrorized discos, clubs, restaurants, smoky little bars, and damn near every bait shack and marina from Manhattan to Cape Hatteras for a host of mysterious reasons, but never for a throw-down. And sure as hell not in Brandeville. He caught the look, and immediately bristled.

"Well, if yowh' gonna git ugly, then the hell witch YEW!"

His Nanny rolled exasperated eyes grandsonward.

"Good Gawdah-mahhty," she sighed, "listen to him—straight up from th'mud rooters in Pawhssum Kingdom!"

In all fairness, though, the South is rife with gracious—although archaic—English. A Roanoke Island matriarch, celebrating her ninety-ninth birthday with five generations of her clan, was "glad to be 'mongst-ye," although she said she "darest not hope to see another great-great-grandchild born"; and a Piedmont-born, Boston-based songwriter once invited a girl in one of his songs to "sit you down besahhd me." On the other hand, an Appalachian mountain woman, surveying a field overflowing with flora, declared there to be "fever-few flowers," which I subsequently learned was a kind of wildflower. I could only surmise, by its name, that it was used in regional folk medicine. All that usage was correct in its time—between the seventeenth and eighteenth centuries—and, funny as it may sound, I had to admit it had a certain timeless elegance to it . . . as well as a lot of color. If budget cuts can "impact" on city services up in Yankeeland, then I imagine a Kentucky creek can "turkey-tail" into little forks down in Dixie. There's no doubt about it; Southerners have elevated the art of descriptive speech beyond flamboyance—sometimes beyond comprehension.

We were coming back to the city marina from the Great South Bay when, quite suddenly, the waves began swelling up in angry troughs, the boat started to pitch, and the sky turned black behind leaden fog. He was having a hard time controlling the wheel, a howling Doberman and a seasick boatboy all at the same time, but he managed, nonetheless, to get us home.

The dock mechanic silently assessed the damage, then shook his head in amazement. "The hull and the rudder have been pounded to hell, and you look like you've had your arms wrenched out. With all that rain and wind crashing down on you, it must have been wild out there!"

He prised his lips from his beer and thought for a minute.

"Yeah," he replied, with deep sincerity, "it was truly hellacious!"

I had to agree with him there. It sho' nuff *was*.

iii. Good Ol' Bawhs At Large

5 A Walk on the Wahhld Sahhd

Southern mores—and therefore, Southern euphemisms—necessitate subtexting. And analysis. This revelation came to me at about two-thirty one morning, when he called to tell me he had felt compelled to avenge an insult from a lifeform so unmentionable, so utterly without saving grace, as to be below even that of Yankee—a difficult distinction to achieve, given the fact that the offender *was* a Yankee. But never mind. As he related it, he'd smacked the guy around a little, and basically let the prostrate gentleman know that he and the bulk of his forebears were pond scum.

"Then," he gloated, "Ah *stomped* him."

I reflected on that momentarily. Surely he didn't mean that he jumped up and down on the guy's ribcage or walked across his back in cleats or, God forbid, kicked him in the head as he lay, helpless, his face ground into the asphalt, grit, and grime. . . .

Or did he?

"No," he grudgingly admitted. His eyes scrunched down into a rabid squint. "But that doan mean he wouldn't'a deserved it if Ah had." Hmmmmmmmm . . .

It was at that point I began formulating my theories on violence and the Southern psyche. I give the sociologists, criminologists, and pop psychologists their due, but there are really very few things that the average Northern Female (or average Northerner, for that matter) needs to know about the subject—and the "why" of it isn't one of them. However, these are:

(1) The Term "Aggravated Assault" Is Redundant.

Of course it is. If some country fool was stupid enough to suggest to you that the Mobile Mud Hens could whip the asses off the Cowboys any old day or night of the week, then of course y'all were perfectly justified in pulling his face off. What kahhnd'a sorry specimen of a may-yan would be dumb enough to both bet against the Cowboys an' 'fess up to it publicly? ("Piss-sant!") Which leads us to:

(2) It's Always Somebody Else's Fault.

All Southern Men, Lawhhd knows, are easy-going, peace-loving, cherubic little humanists who'd rather *dah-hh-h* than raise their hands in violence unto their fellow may-yan. However, should you audibly consider converting to Catholicism. or look the wrong way at His Woman, or even hint that that His Hound Dawg is victim to every congenital defect known to medical science, then your average Southerner is entitled to argue that shooting the legs off of you, *your* Hound Dawg and the woman in question isn't too extreme an action ("she was too good-lookin' foah' her own good anyway"). Likewise, bulldozing the local Catholic church isn't exactly a disgrace, either. Damn thing was an ah-sore, Gawd knows, an' . . . well . . . you know . . . these things jus' git to a may-yan af-tuh a whahl . . .

(3) Retaliation Must Always Be Public, Spectacular, And Totally Disproportionate To The Offense.

Public Revenge has as much to do with Honor as it does Posterity. After all, every legend needs a Boswell. To become a legend, however, one must exact Spectacular Revenge, the kind that is so fierce and original and ingeniously diabolical that it has every Good Ol' Bawh for the next ten counties epileptic with laughter when he attempts to recount it. But—here's the key part—in order to be Spectacular, the Revenge must far and away exceed the enormity of the insult itself. Not only in magnitude, mind you— oh, no; the average New York ax murderer or cult psychotic could easily hack his way through the West Side, and hardly any Manhattanites would blink. No, Disproportionate Revenge must include flair, cunning, and a kind of retribution so exacting that it makes one gasp aloud in eye-rolling awe. It should also be swift, unexpected, and require the participation of as many of one's blood and extended kin as aren't already in jail. It doesn't much matter what sparked the feud, or how long ago it began; the point is that once upon a time, the score was evened up after Somebody Done Somebody Else Wrong.

(4) Somebody ALWAYS Done Somebody Else Wrong.

Drunken Redneck Brawls are okay, but to precipitate true, full-scale internecine warfare, a Glaring Outrage is called for. While Outrages vary in severity, a few sure bets might be, oh, say, telling everyone in town that you know for a fact that all the Skank girls have more mileage on them than their Dai-dy's '53 Buick, that you saw Roscoe Rutledge sneaking out of the Happy Day Beauty Salon in Hawg Hollow, or that Delbert Duke not only doesn't watch any Footbawhl at all, but that he also really did vote for George McGovern—*and* Walter Mondale.

(5) Nevvuh Forget Honor And Self-Righteousness.

Southern Men—unlike New Yorkers—aren't usually inclined to kill for fun, profit, or a parking space; they will, however, cheerfully mangle a person over a point of Honor. This usually has more to do with salt-cured machismo than anything else—Honor, Machismo, and Fearless Fighting being very much a part of their Mythic/Backwoodsman Personae. Fair enough; in those days, not being "much of a man" could mean a death sentence, or at least be cause for major ridicule. But don't overlook the Righteousness Factor; there is no one more self-righteous—be he dirt farmer or televangelist—than a Southerner who thinks he's right. The jaw locks in a deathgrip, the eyebrows furrow into one long, ominous thundercloud, the very eyes of John Calvin blaze three or four centuries of Dissenting Protestant hellfire into the hapless offender—and you are Dahhmmmed!! For all tahhhmm! There's nothing like a little brimstone-eyed conviction to back up one's righteous right arm.

This is why I, for one, get such a kick out of country & western music. All Southerners are marvelous storytellers by birthright, but C/W songs are exceptional in that they always make mention of those elements near and dear to a Good Ol' Bawh's heart—namely, Drinkin' an' Brawlin' an' Ballin' an' Brawlin' an' Drinkin' some more. These, you'll agree, are meaty enough topics in themselves, but what really gets me is their philosophy that every act of carnage wrought by a rampaging Redneck can be justified by blaming it on the next nearest person. A son of the South, jilted by His Su-guh, could probably strafe all of downtown Mobile with mortar fire and get away with it; but should he actually wind up in jail, he would no doubt go to his dying day yelling, "Wouldn't nevvuh have landed heah 'cept that *lahh-yin'* skunk of a woman *put* me heah!"

It's that element of aggrieved self-righteousness that distinguishes Dixie men from their Northern confreres, and if it colors their music and literature, it also colors their humor. Yankee gentlemen, denied the same accepted outlets for mayhem, tantrums, or Spectacular Revenge, usually exact their retribution with the icy efficiency of an overworked coroner—nothing personal, buddy. But an honest-to-God Redneck doesn't care about breaking the crockery, having his credit line evaporate, or being wiped off the Palladium guest list, or any of the ramifications thereof. And it *is* personal—as personal and as powerful to him as his own breathing. He wants his pound of flesh. NOW.

We were watching the news together when there aired a story about a West Virginia miner named Coody Petes, who suspected his girlfriend of carrying on with a fellow miner. It was in one of those tiny, gritty little mining towns where the air hangs, dingy with coal soot, and generations of dour, pinched-faced Scotch-Irish have clawed and scarred the earth, just to be able to eke out a threadbare living. Strange things happen to a lot of men packed into rat-shack housing, with only a few timeworn women around. Coody Petes loaded himself up with two or three sticks of dynamite, stuck a wad of chewing tobacco in his mouth, and walked on over to His Woman's house. Everything went fine—till he accidentally blew himself up.

My Southern Man's reaction was fairly typical.

"Awwwwwwhhh, Coody!" he moaned, "Lawwhhd Gawd Jesus, the woman done you wrawhhhhng!"

My head spun up from my paperwork. "*She* done *him* wrong?" I snarled. "How do you figure that? You don't even know if she was cheating on him, and there he goes—trying to kill her!"

"Ah know, Ah know," he wailed, "poah' Coody, outta his mahhnd with grief an' rage!"

"Poor Coody, my eye!" I spat back. "Coody could've blown up the whole town over his stupid little fit of jealousy!"

He thought about that for perhaps a nanosecond, then began cackling. High, loud, lunatic, fracturing the air into jagged shards: "HAHH! HahhahhahHAHH!"

"You think that's funny?!"

"Naw, it ain't that," he gasped, tears scalding his cheeks, "but look what happened to Coody because of it—oh, Lawwhhd, poah' ol' Coody!" He was doubled over on the rug now, his head smacking the floor with each convulsion, as the Dawg began to yowl uncertainly. I couldn't take any more.

"Just what, then, is so hilarious?" I hissed at him. "This is downright gruesome!"

He wiped his eyes, soothed the Dawg, and knifed me on a menacing glare.

"Yeah," he allowed, "Ah suppose. But think upon this: if Coody were wrong, then he gawhht what he desuhhved. But if Coody were right—" he paused, stuck out his chin, and extracted his cigarette from his teeth, "at least he dahhd lahhk a *May-yan*." He started to cackle all over again. "Be-sahhds, they only found but one piece'a Coody aftuh his pants blew up. . . . " He grinned, savoring the moment immensely. "So, can you imagine what that cheatin' dawg of a woman did when they handed her Coody's backbone ahn' said, ' 'Scuse me, ma'm, but Coody would want you to have *this*' !"

My private guess is that she never looked at another male human being again. My grit-fed guru, however, had the last word.

"Coody done left this world a suhti-fahhd legend," he sighed, "an' he sho' nuff dahhd lahhk a *May-yan!*"

And I guess, when you get down to it, that that's all the Coody Petes of the world could ever ask for.

Except, possibly, getting their spinal columns back.

6 *No Place Lahhk Home*

It has occurred to me—more than once—that Southerners are basically schizophrenic. The first time this happened was when he went through his closet and discovered his ex-roommate had absconded with some of his clothes.

"Sumbitch," he seethed, "Ah'm gonna whip that bawh's ass. Then Ah'm gonna cut him awhf at th'knees."

My eyes never moved from the *New York Times* crossword.

"Mmmm-hmmmm," I acknowledged. "But first, how about calling him and giving him a chance to return them? You shared clothes for over three years, after all."

The curtains froze to the walls and the Dawg fled, howling, as a glacial eye glinted nastily from the depths of the closet. Truly, the man had a future in cryogenics.

"I guess not, huh?"

He straightened to his full six feet and bit his toothpick in half with a snap.

"What Ah guess," he informed me, "is if some smart-ass Yankee girl wants to go out foah' that seven-course dinnuh t'nahht, she'd best hush up and let *the men* sort out *th'men's* problems."

I bestowed an angelic smile upon him. "Seven courses," I cooed, "that would be a six-pack and a dead possum, right?"

He jabbed a warning finger at me. "Steve first—then you." And loped out the door.

This is what I mean about schizophrenia. Fifteen minutes earlier, he and Steve had been blood-brothers, inseparable—devout drinking buddies who sailed, fished, swam, partied, and, of course, drank together, who had shared a room together until the day Steve moved out. Steve had even done what no woman had been able to do before or since—he had come between that Southern Man and his Hound Dawg. I guessed that the late Hodding Carter may have been right, after all: A Southerner will generally be polite—even elaborately warm and generous—until he is angry enough to kill you.

It must come from the insularity. Life for Americans in the big Northern cities expanded outward, in a rush; but the South remained, for a long time, basically a collection of tribal villages close, as Marshall Frady wrote, to the skin and the simple heats of mortality, close and connected and very much part of everything that makes a person human—be it love, hate, passion, greed, jealousy, happiness, anger, loyalty, or faith. Or vengeance. Emotion, to a son of the South, runs as close to the surface as his own veins. A Good Ol' Bawh is someone who can, with no apparent contradiction, kill a dozen people with over-potent rotgut, and then scream about AIDS being a PLO plot to undermine American manhood; he can march his children off to church to have it pounded into them that All Men Are Brothers, and then just as easily help lynch the local high school janitor for offenses real or imagined—or just on principle. And he can happily watch three generations of his clan marry into a neighboring one and— just like the Hatfields and the McCoys—butcher the bulk of them over the years in a fit of interfamily pique.

The first call came in around 7:30 P.M.

"Ah cay-yan't take you out rahht now," he rumbled. I smiled to myself and picked up *War and Peace*. "Let me guess," I purred, "you and Clint Eastwood are painting the town red."

"Very funny."

"Charles Bronson?"

He snarled rabidly down the phone. "Ah jus' wanted t'tell you that th'bail money's bah th'bedroom lamp."

"Oh," I chirped, "and your lawyer's number?"

"Good-BAH!!" he spat.

The next one came in at 9:30 P.M.

"It's Steve," the voice declared. "Where's the boyfriend?"

"Out killing Yankees," I said helpfully. "And you're one of them."

I could hear Steve suck in his breath in shock, then exhale nervously. "But I'm an Arizonan!" he protested.

"You," I told him, "are a *dead* Arizonan."

"Oh shit," he gasped, "'Bye!"

"G'bye . . . "

The third one came a half-hour later.

"Found the piss-ant," he cackled. "He's ovvah bah th'bar, knee-deep in othuh sissies to protect his sorry ass."

"He knows you want him," I said.

"Yeah? Well it won't do him no good." He cackled again—strange, evil, electric. "*Dahhh*, you mis'rable swahn! You can run, but you cay-yan't hide!"

The fourth one was from Steve again.

"Are you sure he's mad at me?" he asked. "He came over here about an hour ago, and has been buying me drinks ever since."

"Are you sure you didn't accidentally-on-purpose borrow some of his clothes?" I replied.

"Oh . . . "

"'Oh' is right."

Click.

I had briefly entertained the notion that my erstwhile bar-brawler had suddenly changed his mind, invoked eight years of friendship, and amicably requested that his clothes be returned. I based this on the proven knowledge that I wasn't, as a rule, given to flights of fantasy—especially where he was concerned. But hell . . . I'd been wrong before . . . like I was now.

"Nailed the sumbitch!" he crowed. I sighed into the mouthpiece as he exulted onward. "Got him wasted out of his brains and conned him outside. We were damn near a block away befoah' Ah let him have it."

"Did you kill him, by chance?" I inquired sweetly.

"Naw," he confessed, with just a tinge of disappointment. "Jus' smacked him upsahd th'head a little." He paused, wounded integrity in his voice. "He's mah *brothuh*, f'Gawd's sake!"

Oh . . . right.

The call-waiting signal beeped down the line. It was Steve.

"He's killed me!" he screamed. "I have a concussion, two black eyes, a split lip, and my jaw's loose! I think he's broken my ribs!"

"I see," I commented, all business. "Where are you now?"

"In the phone booth down the block from the bar."

I went back to the other line. "He's where you left him," I said, "and he thinks he's dying."

"Shit, he ain't dahh-yin'," he growled. "But he probably wishes he was. Doan worry—I'll take care of him."

"That," I pointed out, "is just what I was afraid of."

I was therefore somewhat startled to see the front door break off its hinges as he, with Steve draped across a shoulder, came staggering into the living room about a half-hour later.

"Lookit him," he cooed, oozing worry, "he doan look too good. Not too good at all."

"Uh-huh," I acknowledged. "Steve's a mess, all right."

"Shit," he replied. "Lookit—y'all won't be able to tek a decent head shot of him foah'... days. Weeks, maybe."

Steve moaned mournfully. "You've ruined my life, you Visigoth!"

"Poah' little sumbitch," his antagonist soothed back. "Here— y'get a steak foah' your eye, an' a little ah-oh-dahhn foah' them cuts—"

"You've wrecked my face!" Steve wailed. "I'll never model again!"

"—an' some moah' on your knuckles, rahht?"

Steve sighed tiredly. "Right. Iodine."

"Uh-huh. Give you some Ambesawhl foah' your teeth—"

"Oh, yeah, Ambesol—"

"—an' have th'folks at Roosevelt x-ray them ribs—"

"A little tape, maybe—"

"Yeah, tape." He paused, disappeared into the bedroom, and re-emerged with an assortment of pill bottles. "You want sumthin' foah' th' pain?"

"Oh... some brandy, I guess... "

"Brandy," he winced, and strolled over to the bar. "Sumbitch wants *brandy*."

"VSOP... Remy Martin, perhaps—"

"Lookit!" exclaimed his would-be nurse, "he wants Remy Mah-tahhhn! Sorry fool sho' nuff knows how to get his ass beat up!" He hesitated fractionally, then flipped a steak on to broil. "May as well have one foah' your stomach, too."

"Medium rare, please," Steve said. I thought maybe he'd pushed the other man too far this time, but he just gritted his teeth and adjusted the heat. "Medium rare," he mumbled.

Steve arose and crawled off towards the bedroom. "I have to lie down," he emoted. "You *will* bring it to me, won't you?"

I decided, suddenly, that it would be a propitious moment to walk the Dawg. To New Jersey. He, however, just handed Steve his cognac and eyed him pointedly. "Yeah, buddy," he muttered, "Ah reckoned we *could*."

It was some time before I got up the nerve to sound him out. "I can't figure you out," I told him. "You damn near beat your best friend to death over some sweaters, and now, all of a sudden, you're his personal valet and wet nurse. You have a chemical imbalance, or what?"

He turned glittering dark eyes on me and chortled. "Naw, it ain't a chemical imbalance or sumthin'. An' yeah, I damn near did kill him, but Ah damn near do love that bawh, too. Steve—" he called. The older man came over.

"You ain't evvah gonna touch mah clothes again, are you?"

"No way!" he swore.

"An' you'll see to it Ah get these ones back, won't you?"

"You bet."

"Aw, hell, Steve, y'all kin have 'em, anyway."

"Oh . . . well . . . thanks," he stammered. "Thanks a lot."

"Now, get back t'bed."

He watched Steve disappear back into the bowels of the bedroom, and laughed shortly to himself. "Thass awhll," he said, mussing my hair. "You Yankees," he groaned. "It was jus' sumthin' a May-yan had t'do." He looked me straight in the eye, shrugged, and grinned good-naturedly. "It wa'n't nuthin' personal."

And resumed the excavation of his closet.

It is that series of inherently contradictory impulses that, I believe, make Southerners so colorful. They can be the most altruistic, community-minded people on God's earth, but they still love a good feud—preferably one in which they can blissfully indulge for, oh, a generation or so. They can also be some of the most upright, virtuous, and devout churchgoers this side of the Reformation, and still gleefully gloat about how they excommunicated their fellow Baptist Brother Kendall for drunkenness and wife-beating—just five minutes after Conference. And they are the first ones to scream bloody murder about the rights of an individual being trampled on, then go out and fire-bomb the house of the local Socialist.

It has, as I said, everything to do with insularity. No matter how much the New South begins to look like New Jersey or Long Island or any place in Middle America, it's reassuring to know that the people themselves will never by anything else but uniquely Southern—regardless of the inroads made by TV, superhighways, education or assimilation. The New Southerners of today seem to have effortlessly straddled two divergent worlds—again, without apparent contradiction. You can get cordon bleu cuisine in Charlottesville or Charleston or Raleigh, and you can buy the same shirt in Miller & Rhoads in Richmond, as in Bullock's in Atlanta, as you can in Macy's in New York. But even more telling than those facts are some of the observations made by various journalists, historians, and sociologists. For instance, as John Shelton Reed wrote in his book, *The Enduring South*:

* Bob Jones University has a program specifically designed for the modern churchman—a course in "missionary aviation."

* A Georgia radio station airs a live show hosted by an announcer named John Wesley Cohen.

* A newspaper recipe column reports that beaten biscuits are undergoing a renaissance, since homemakers and bakers across Dixie discovered they could be made with a food processor—instead of wooden mallets.

However, the most telling item that comes to mind, whenever I start worrying that the Eastern Corridor will gradually swell out and swallow the South, uniqueness, insularity, and all, is the thought once scrawled on a wall in Chapel Hill:

U.S. OUT OF NORTH CAROLINA

The South will never rise again.
Because it never fell.

7 *Y'all Come Back Real Soon, Now*

Hospitality is an interesting facet of human nature. I thought maybe the Italian and Jewish mothers of New York had cornered the market on warmth and killing a person with kindness, but that was before I headed south one winter. Before I left, though, I asked my friend Ron about the last time he went home, to Alabama.

He stopped typing long enough to give me a flat, unfocused stare.

"You know why Southerners never return home?" he asked.

"Because they hate to leave once they get there?"

"No-o-oo-o," he moaned, his eyes suddenly snapping back into orbit, "because the folks won't never let you *go-o-oo-oo!*"

He shoved his scripts aside and took my hand. "You don't understand," he said. "When I was a boy, my parents sent me from Montgomery to stay with my great-aunt Fanny for a few weeks one summer. Aunt Fanny and my uncle, and all these ancient, ancient people lived way up in the Florida Panhandle, *wa-a-aa-ayy* at the end of this long, dusty dirt road . . . high up in nowhere. And they left me there. *All* summer." He fumbled for a cigarette, and struggled to compose himself. "*With* Aunt Fanny. And my uncle. And all these strange, wild, funny-sounding . . . relatives. An' Ah'll nevvuh fo'-get," he whispered, his accent fracturing dangerously into Southern, "that this woman drove me down that endless dirt road . . . an' suddenly, she comes to a screeching hawhlt! Ahn' do you know *whah*?"

I chewed my lip thoughtfully. "Dead revenuer in the road, perhaps?"

"Worse," Ron wailed, "a *lahhvv* armadillo!"

I couldn't quite see why the appearance of an armadillo in the middle of Mangrove Central should be such an alarming occurrence; one walking up Sixth Avenue, yes; but one cropping up between the Mojave and northern Florida, no. Still . . .

"It was horrible," he murmured. "She leapt rahht out of th'car, pulled a baseball bat outta th' trunk, an' smacked that thing clear to Tallahassee!"

"Why?" I demanded. "Was it dangerous?"

"No-o-ooo," Ron moaned again, "it was *sup-puh*!"

He put his face in his hands and shuddered. "The woman stood there with this dahhhmm armadillo swingin' bah th'tail an' sez, 'Le's stop off at Eula n' Cecil's so she kin cook it up rahht now fo' our Ron!' An armadillo! Fo' me!" He groaned loudly and rolled anguished brown eyes up to mine. "Nuthin' was too much trouble, fo' her little city relative. That woman clocked the poah' thing cold, drove us thirty mahhls outta th'way to show it—an' me—off to Eula an' Cecil an' awhwhl the half-cousins, an' then slung the gawddahhmm animal in a pot t'simmuh. She had that thing put up by six o'clock."

I handed Ron his coffee and patted his shoulder, hoping he'd let the memory go; but he fixed his eyes on me a final time and rasped, "Do you have any idea what stewed armadillo *smells* lahhk? I smelled armadillo an' swamp an' things Ah doan even wanna think about *awhhl summuh lawwwhhng*. An' that dear, dear woman couldn't hardly do enough fo' her kin. Me. An' *thass* whah," he rapped out, "Suth'nuhs nevvuh go home!"

His point was well taken. I remember heading over to the house of a kinsman of my Southerner's tribe, and discovering one particularly salient feature of the Southern personality: namely, that being friendly and hospitable—"neighborly," in their terminology—was not so much a question of inviting people over, as it was just *going* over. And you couldn't "drop by for just a minute," either; the food would start arriving, almost of its own volition, and you could easily spend the next two, three, even four hours on the doorstep saying goodbye—

"Y'all just cay-yan't run awhhf lahhk that so soon, now!" —and then be loaded down with so many goodies you couldn't move if you wanted to.

And then there was the Christmas at his parents' house. The pantry, kitchen table, and every spare inch of counter space was already groaning under the weight of breads, cakes, pies, and anything that could feasibly be pickled or canned—and still His Mama cooked. And cooked. And cooked some more. I couldn't take it any longer.

"Who are you cooking for, the Confederate Army?"

His Mama batted her eyelashes blandly. "Whah, jus' th'family," she purred. She smiled, Mona Lisa–like. "'Case they get peckish."

"She gawwhna need it," Her Mama interjected. "You ain't met Big yet." I closed my eyes resignedly. "Big?"

"Big," Nanny assured me.

I tried a different tack. "What's Big's real name?"

Nanny thought about that for perhaps five minutes; turned to her eldest daughter, who turned to her sister—Big's wife—who bit her lip for another five minutes.

"Ah doan know," Alice finally said, her voice tiny. "'least, Ah doan remember. He always been jus'... jus'..."

"*Big*," said their Mama.

"*Big*," seconded her daughters.

And he was. To say the least. It wasn't so much that he was tall, really, or fat—he was just massive. I knew, when the light died abruptly in the living room, when the front doorjambs creaked and the floors began to shake, that Big, indeed, had arrived. Darkness at high noon. Hands like suitcases.

My Southern Male was ecstatic. "He a good guy, is Big," he said. "But Mama gawwht a real nice touch with him, anyway. Jus' in case."

I looked over to see her hand Big a whole carved turkey. "Theah's yowhs, honey," she told him, "jus' put it on th'table whahl Ah fetch up th'othuh one."

Big beamed pure sunshine upon his sister-in-law, and ambled off. I thought I heard a low laugh underneath that thick, black outrage of beard and moustache, but I couldn't be totally sure.

Hospitality is probably the Southerner's greatest trait. When the frontier was young and wild and wide-open generations ago, and homesteads were few and far between, it would have been unthinkable not to offer food and shelter to the passing traveler, and equally unthinkable and un-Christian not to help a neighbor in need. This was how the South survived, from the antebellum era on through the years of the Depression—and is, to some extent, how they still do it today. The necessity for such hospitality may have diminished somewhat, but the compulsion to give, to share, and to do it so freely and graciously, still thrives—as does the instinct to pull together, as a community. Perhaps it's got less to do with everybody being related to each other—however distantly—than it does with everybody knowing one another. I once heard an ancient great-grandmother in Tupelo, Mississippi, personally name nearly everyone in the entire town, right down to the youngest toddler.

Which is not to say Southerners don't guard their privacy. They are too tough, too independent, and too self-reliant not to. A friend of mine, riding in the Georgia hills, inadvertently strayed into the bastion of a notoriously antisocial mountain clan named Lowry. The family was something of a mystery; a hundred years earlier, some rangy Lowry took His Woman up the hill, and busied himself begetting heirs and fortifying his aerie. The rumor therefore went that the denizens of Lowry Mountain were stump-toothed, inbred, half-deranged throwbacks that somehow arose from the antediluvian ooze and adapted to land—not unlike the hillbillies of *Deliverance*—seeing as how no fresh blood had been introduced into the tribe in the entire course of the century. In any case, the Lowrys were up there, in full force: a truly verminous race of ridge runners, who devoted the bulk of their copious leisure time to making whiskey, salt-pork, and even more children. And my drinking buddy had strode right into the midst of them.

"Well, it wasn't too bad," he said. "They all had this mean, half-wahhld look about 'em—you know, kind'a craggy, rawbone . . . Appalachian faces. But I can't say Ah was really terrifahd until their Daddy spoke up."

"Why?" I asked. "What did he say?"

My friend laughed and smiled nervously. "He pointed a 12-gauge at me and said, 'Stranguh, doan let th'sun set awhhn you heah.'"

"And?"

"And," he told me, "Ah *didn't*."

I could picture that. The South was full of warnings similar to that, right on up through the '60s. Reporters covering the Civil Rights movement in Dixie were frequently confronted with motel signs that ran something like:

> NO REPORTERS
> NO DOGS
> NO NIGGERS

as well as the usual complement of snarling canines, lynch mobs, and the ubiquitous 12-gauge. In all fairness, though, that came during the height of what was a national agony for both blacks and whites, for both Northerners and Southerners, and is probably best laid to rest now. We can all live without that. But it's that feisty, indomitable quality about rednecks that I grudgingly admire—something to do with an occasional brittle snap in the eye, and a defiant bulldog jut to the jaw that says y'all mahht-a whipped that bawh's ass this tahhm, but he's *still* better than you anyhow. And a certain wild, reckless grin they grin that says they're never really beaten—because they never give up. Not an inch. That's why I don't doubt there are still some rough pockets of the ruffian South left—because there still are some ruffian *Southerners* left.

We were about to sit down to dinner one night in New York, when the phone suddenly rang. It was his best friend, Clay. My saltpork-sired sweetheart listened intently for a few minutes, grunted, then hung the phone up, expressionless.

"Clay jus' sawed his leg awhhff," he reported.

I dropped the béarnaise sauce. "He what?"

"Sawed his leg awhhff," he repeated blandly. He stabbed his filet mignon. "Good steak, darlin',"

I gaped at him in shock. "A man just amputated his own leg," I stammered. "How can you be so *emotionless* about that? Your best friend!"

He eyed me without moving a single muscle of his face. "Oh, he's awwhraht," he assured me, "it was only one leg."

I threw my napkin across the room and fried him on a lively volt of hate-filled electricity. "I'm not entirely sure of this," I hissed, "but I think I hate you."

He gave me a slow, saintly smile. "Ah doan think you quite understahhn'," he explained, ever so sweet, ever so patient. Now I was sure I hated him. "Clay is a Good Ol' Bawh. He'll pull through. He was conscious and cussing out them gawddahhm Yankee doctuhs all th'way inta surgery. They had t'strap th'sumbitch down jus' to anesthe-tahhz him!" He paused, and peered at me questioningly. "You know what he was fussin' about?"

I couldn't imagine.

His face split into leathery dimples as he cackled, "He was pissed awhf 'cause he thought th'piss-ants done fawh-gawwht t'bring his leg alawhng with 'em!"

I felt my bile backing up. He put his cutlery down and took my hand, all anxious concern.

"What's th'mattuh, honey?," he cooed, "steak gawwhn bad?" He slept by himself that night. On the couch.

He crashed through the front door about a week later, laughing hysterically. "You'll nevvuh guess what happened!" he whooped, "Clay's outta th'hawspital!"

"So soon?" I wondered. "The man nearly died!"

"Nearly, but not quite!" He pulled himself off the floor, and clutched me around the knees. "Them doctuhs had poah' Clay awwhhl wired with tubes an' oxygen an' shit, an' he jus' couldn't take it no moah'. So he waits until he's alone an' the ICU hall-way's fairly quiet, unplugs himself, an' wheels himself out 'n' down to Nahhnth Avenue!" Another paroxysm of hysteria seized him. He laughed so hard, he started spitting his tooth caps out. I rolled my eyes up into my hairline and waited.

"Clay wheeled hi'self rahht awhn to th' street, caught a cab, an' went straight home to five, six fingers of home-brewed bour-bon!"

Oh, no. No way. Not even a mean, tough old buzzard of a red-neck like Clayton.

"Oh, yes," my Southern Man swore, "he sho' did! Yes, m'am! I wouldn'a believed it mahself, 'cept Ah saw a trail of shell-shocked nurses an'orduhlies strung from Intensive Care awhhl th'way awhn down to th'main lobby. He musta taken a few bahhts outta that crowd, an' then blew away. Ohhh, Gawwhhd, Ah thought Ah'd done ruptured sumthin' laffin' mahself sick!" He mopped the tears off his face, shook his head, and laughed some more. "Oh, Jesus, Clay! Ohhhhhh, mon—what a May-yan, Lawwwhhhd! What a May-yan! Oh, Clay! Oh, mon!"

Of such men are moonshine runners and desperados made. I listened to this monologue for a minute—this strange combina-tion of menace, insanity, and fragmentary coherence that wreaks havoc on the mind of the sane listener—and then picked up the phone. "You better call him and make sure he isn't a *dead* 'may-yan,'" I told him.

His eyes shot sparks. "Chile, there ain't but one way you kin kill awwhhf a Suth'un bawh," he rumbled, "an' thass to cut awhhff his haid an' shrink it." He put the phone back down and cackled, teeth gleaming. "Be-sahhds, we gonna see ol' Clay in a little whahl."

He pulled a few bottles of Yankee whiskey out of the liquor cabinet, and lugged a crate of Heinekens to the front door. I buried my face in my hands and gave up right then. I knew why we were going over to Clay's, and I knew it would involve about fifty or sixty Good Ol' Bawhs, several well-upholstered females, and as much booze as we could transport across town without a state license or a police escort.

"Yeahhh," my Southern Male cheerfully confirmed, "good ol' legless, cut-up Clay wants to thank us-awhhl foah' bein' so neighbuhly, he's up an' throwin' hi'self a party!"

And inviting, no doubt, damn near all of New York.

8 *The Cawhhl of the Wahhld*

Camping, I have found, brings out the worst in a man. It's bad enough when, on your own turf, you get shouldered aside so he can probe the depths of the car's engine, change a lightbulb, or attempt to solve any other one of a score of highly technical problems, but just pointing him in the general direction of the Great Outdoors is infinitely worse—because then you have Gunga Din Goes Backpacking on your hands.

This is true of all men, but Southern Men take their rugged frontier efficiency to ruthless lengths. New Yorkers recognize this as the ¿Que Es Macho? Effect; my friend George, however, more accurately identified it as The *Deliverance* Syndrome.

You know how that works. Their eyes get a mean metallic glint to them, their eyebrows split their foreheads in one long, fierce slash, and they start chewing imaginary wads of tobacco, jamming their hands into their back pockets, and rocking on their heels. "Woman," they bark, "fetch me mah knaff, mah gun, an' mah Dawg." This, from a man in Topsiders and a polo shirt.

The first time it happened, I froze in my tracks. "Woman"? "Kna-aff"? "Dawg"?!! What the hell happened to "sweetheart," "car keys," and "Walkman"—words I understood? I studied him frostily.

"You," I informed him, "don't have a Dawg. Yet."

He thought about that one.

"Well," he murmured, "kin Ah borruh yowh' cat?"

All men are Southerners when it comes to camping.

But, as I said, Southern Men are worse. The man could have been born and bred in downtown Miami and schooled at Yale, but he will still insist on telling you more than you ever wanted to know about skinning possum, gutting fish, and staking tent pegs. This knowledge, I am now sure, is congenital, passed on down through the male line like a degenerative nerve disease. There is no other explanation—logical or otherwise—for an apparently civilized, housebroken, adult male to suddenly lose command of his syntax, grammar, and senses in general, and go roughing it in the Appalachian outback. I thought it might have something to do with nostalgia: you know, the sweet, sad haze of romantic pseudo-history that every Southerner gets dewy-eyed over. . . . But there is actually a far more subversive purpose to Roughing It, a vile, creeping malaise so insidious it is, at first, barely discernable—it's the dreaded Instant Expert Syndrome.

You get a taste of that almost immediately. First of all, you're on His Turf, which means he is, in theory, intimately acquainted with all the flora, fauna, and other wildlife of the region; second, he speaks the language; and third, he is a Southern, bah Gawwd, May-yan!, which automatically makes him infinitely more capable than that poah' little inept-but-well-meaning Yankee girl, heh-heh-heh-heh! You get a sense, right away, that this is going to be a Long Trip.

It was. We were trying to set up and stake a tent one evening high in the Blue Ridge Mountains, through stinging sheets of rain. Setting up a tent for the first time is unnerving enough, but doing so in the midst of a howling hurricane with a rabid Southerner at hand can only be likened to finding yourself in shark territory during a feeding frenzy . . . there are no winners or losers, only survivors.

"Peel the flahh awhf an' put it unduh th'tree!" he screamed, jabbing at the ground. I looked around frantically for something that might be a fly—a fishing line, a small black thing, airplane wings—anything. Nothing.

"The *flah*! The *flah*!" he shrieked again. His eyes squirted blood as his brain boiled over with pent-up toxins. Truly, he was a tad upset. "The whahht tawhhp!"

I peered groundward nervously. A large, shapeless, bone-colored mass lay pooled at my feet. Oh. I grabbed it and ran.

"Now thread th'tent-poles through th'loops—UNDUH th'cross-poles—in an ehh-yex. . . . awwwwhh, shee-yit!" He ripped the elasticized metal tubes out of my hands, snapping them like brittle spaghetti. I watched in horror as he rammed them into their loops, nearly tearing the tent.

"Now bow them."

That was easy enough. You stretch the tent over the flexible rods, which are then bent and locked into metal sockets, bowing the tarpaulin of the tent into shape. It was built like a teardrop, split in half and laid sideways. He called it The Enviro-dome; I called it The Egg.

"Now we do the flahh."

Flies work just like the tent itself, so we got through that maneuver with little comment on our respective origins, intellects, or parentages. It was, however, almost nightfall before I could bring myself to ask him about the naming of the fly.

He pointed to its outermost tip, jutting over the doorflap like a Dover cliff.

"See?" he enthused, "See how it flahhhs?"

I studied the tarp wordlessly, trying to picture its aerodynamic properties. I gave up.

"It's so obvious," he sneered, "how could you miss it?"

We hardly spoke for the next few days.

In time, though, I learned all about Camping Lore. Not only the names of brackets, sprockets, pins, zips, rods, and a slew of other things that already had perfectly understandable names, but also about Mountain Lore—how to repel mosquitoes without bug spray, building fires, tracking animals, edible vegetation, and numerous other facts that would, no doubt, prolong my life and ease my days in the wilds of Manhattan.

But I persevered, and if my affection for him didn't increase, my respect for him did. I had had, after all, several weeks of survival training prior to the Great Roadtrip—how to lash up a backpack, how to balance loads, finding water in the Appalachian wilderness, Meeting And Greeting Large Starving Bears—and I began to develop utter faith in this man. He was thorough, knowledgeable, and efficient, to an excruciating degree. . . . He was saturated with the wisdom of ages, steeped in the secrets of wilderness survival; a worthy flame-carrier of the generations of pioneers and frontiersmen who had gone before him and tamed the land. . . . He was also being a creep. But I stood in awe of him, nonetheless.

Until . . . The Trek.

We filled up on water, smeared ourselves with insect repellent, balanced our packs and tied on our bandanas. He made a last check of the pack straps, lashed up the sleeping bags, and made sure his home blend of trail mix would last into the next hollow. Satisfied, he stopped to drink in the soft, rolling hills. A sleepy peace suffused his face, his eyes half-closing in comatose contentment. He was one with the woods, one with the mountains, one with his heritage once again. At long last, my salt-cured sensei spoke up.

"There's jus' one thing Ah need to know," he murmured, drowsily.

I waited for him to tell me his thoughts, confide his dreams, expound on the meaning of life, or ponder the majesty and mystery of the mountains.

"What?" I sighed, hanging on to his every breath.

"Jus' one thing . . . "

"What?" I whispered. "Tell me. . . . "

He cracked open a lazy eye.

"What does poison ah-vy look lahhk?"

He fled, screaming, through some of it and down the hill, as I clocked him cold with a full two-quart water bottle. *¿Que Es Macho?*, my eye!!

And I've never watched "The Waltons" since.

9 *Awhhl Things Brahht an' Beautiful*

New York City is not, you'd probably agree, a fisherman's first choice of fishing holes. Not even his second or third. Oh, sure, you can charter a boat in Sheepshead Bay or sneak off to Long Island or even run with whatever is biting off of Sandy Hook, but by and large, fishing tackle and go-go Gothamites do not coexist side by side in Manhattan.

Which is enough of a reason in itself for me to love the place. Whatever else life in New York threw at me, I was reasonably sure it would at least not involve bait, middle-of-the-night mornings, and foul-smelling boyfriends encased in rubber made fouler by fish guts and scales. Don't get me wrong—I grew up riding, running, and swimming. I had hiked, trekked, and climbed the Himalayan foothills in my time, so I wasn't exactly the retiring kind; but there is something about a fish thrashing on the end of a line, about the smell of brine and slime and things in buckets that I can't identify but which fishermen call Bait, that is enough to send me fleeing to the nearest penthouse with a half-dozen videocassettes of "Miami Vice."

Fishing, naturally, is a sacred Southern pastime, a form of recreation pursued purely for its own sake rather than for business, social, or therapeutic reasons. It's part of the Rugged Outdoorsman/Original Aboriginal Grit mentality which, even now, compels twentieth-century, middle-aged insurance salesmen from suburban Mechanicsville to strap on their gear, pack their equipment, round up the Dawgs and tell their wives, "Woman, Ah'm goin' inta th'wahlds." Pause. "See y'all in two, three weeks." These are the same men who labored for years, to get themselves out of the gray, gritty little towns that have top-notch places to fish in that they now flee back to at every opportunity so that their sons don't grow up deprived. It may not be as macho as, say, hunting, but it's every bit as important. It is a spiritual thing, as much as it is environmental or psycho-cultural.

It's also a very serious business. We were near Blue Bend, West Virginia, when the urge to drop a line into the nearest creek suddenly came upon him.

"This is going to be a little tricky," I cautioned, "considering we're in mountain country. Just where do you expect to get ahold of some bait?"

"No problem," he replied, "we'll jus' head awhn ovvuh t' th'nearest grocery stawh."

I felt the gray folds of my brain wince, mightily, like an accordion suddenly being slammed shut. What in hell could he buy as bait from a little old country store? Bread? Hell, no; even if they stocked Wonder Bread. These were Southern fish we were dealing with and probably wouldn't touch "light bread," as these people so gleefully called it. Anchovies? Olives? Not likely. This wasn't exactly Zabar country, and you could hardly expect to find the funny foreign food that Yankees habitually ingest Up Nawwhth, with no apparent fear over stomach erosion or brain damage. No, no chance of that. Not in West, bah Gawd, Vahginnyuh! What bait, then?

"Cockroaches," he said simply.

Roaches. Oh, God. *Las Cucarachas*. Those horrible little indestructibles that all New Yorkers are raised, from birth, to seek out, destroy, and otherwise wreak havoc with. Roaches. Being stored, *alive*, among the eggs and the cheese and ham and milk and vegetables. My skin turned bilious as I hung my head out the car window.

"Tell me you're joking," I croaked.

He wasn't. We strolled into the Paradise General Supply

Store, and there they were—some dead, some alive, but all neatly contained in a variety of little glass jars with tiny airholes punched through the lids. Little itsy bitsy roaches for, I guess, minnowy kinds of fish, and big, husky ones damn near the size of carpet slippers. Roaches. I heard my stomach churn over.

"Ah'll tek an assortment," he told the owner. The older man glanced at the younger one mutely.

"Th'daid ones are easier to hook," my beloved explained. "Less chance of upsetting mah lady-girl heah."

"Oh, sho' thang," agreed the storekeeper, "them bugs aren't for everbody. But," he added, profering a huge, dark brown one, "they's jes' *bugs*."

"Not if you're from New Yawwhk," my mate replied.

"Ohhhh," said the mountain man, "one of *those*." I smiled tightly. He turned kind green eyes on me and beamed me a high-wattage smile. "Maybe y'all could ship me a few hundred when y'git back home?"

"Sure," I purred. My fishing buddy threw me a warning glance. I blinked innocently. "Sprayed or unsprayed?"

"Doan matter," said the grocer, "jes' as lawhhng as they big an' tough an' not too mean."

I had a brief vision of having to interview my quarry to ascertain their ruggedness ("You sumo wrestle? Chase dogs? Move parked cars?"), but instantly shrugged it off.

"Not too . . . *mean*?"

"Yeahhh," he drawled. "They got t'be big enough and hard enough to stay on th'hook, but not so rowdy y'all cay-yan't handle them."

"I see," I squeaked. "I'll do my best."

"Good!" he grinned. "Ah jes' hate a rowdy cockroach."

Don't we all.

In any case, we got our bait, and headed for the nearest creek. "Cricks," I found, are absolutely necessary to the emotional well-being of Dixie-bred men, but if you can't come by a crick or swimmin' hole, a "run" will have to do. I never discovered what exactly the difference is between a crick and a run, except, possibly, that a crick is a little wider or deeper; I did learn, however, that they both must be colder than an ice floe in the Bering Strait—cold, even in August. At high noon. That way, when your Southern Man accidentally drops one of his precious damn roaches in the water for the third time, you can be soggy and frozen as well as surly as a rabid badger. No fishing trip would be complete without that.

I had hoped, once we got back towards civilization, that the fishing fever would subside, and we could then go back to our normal, pleasant vacation routine, like trying to start a fire in the driving rain, listening for starved bobcats, and skinning squirrels for dinner. Things that all genteelly-raised Yankee ladies are bred for. But no. We were almost back to the Virginia state line, and there was still a glint of *poisson* passion lurking evilly in his eyes.

"Girl," he said, "let's look for a bait stawh."

Oh, no, not again. Not for an even bigger, roachier place, no doubt crawling, wall-to-wall, with the things. I could just see these specialized bait shacks with giant roach heads mounted on plaques on the wall, or whole roaches stuffed by the local taxidermist and placed strategically throughout the place—"Fergus, hatched May '84 . . . he was a good'un"; "Maybell, spawned 2 million champion fish-catchers"; or "Lucinda, took three big Dawgs to bring her down"—the kind of thing Manhattanites have nightmares about. Uggggh.

"Naw, naw," he reassured me. "Those are only in the little ol' country stawhs. We're goin' inta th'town bait shops. Real hahhtech."

And it was. It was the Spread The Word Christian Book Store And Bait Shop. I had to look twice to make sure I wasn't hallucinating.

"Yeah, well, we only have but 231 people in this heah town," said the proprietor, "so we kinda had t'double up our inventory." He grinned wildly, like an ingenuous crocodile. "Salvation an' recreation in one shot!"

He had a point. Truly, the Good Word was providing a noble and outstanding service for the community, for, right opposite the glossy hymnals, the brand-new editions of the King James Bible and the "Virginians—God's Chosen People" bumper stickers, ran racks and shelves and bins fairly groaning with tackle and gear and all-weather clothing—and bait. Not only pails of worms, but lizards, too, and nightcrawlers and grubs and larvae in various stages. I couldn't help but be impressed, knowing full well, as I did, that crickets—not roaches—are the Southern fisherman's favorite bait of choice. Still, you make do with what you've got, and both Paradise's and The Good Word's approach to the fresh bait supply/demand problem was, if nothing else, rather ingenious. At least The Good Word had avoided stockpiling roaches.

"How is the neighborhood preacher taking this?" I asked.

"Fahhn," he replied. "Came in an' blessed th'place when we expanded."

"His side or yours?"

"Both," he said, without missing a beat. "But we had th'reggiler Sunday mawhnin' fishin' bawhs say a few wuhhds ovvuh th'fishin' rods jus' in case."

Richmond, Virginia, never looked so good to any Yankee since the Union Army marched on it during the War, as it looked to me the day we breezed into downtown. Here, finally, I might be safe from the onslaught of mountain-bred roaches and town-bred crawlers and men in plaid shirts lugging beer coolers and fishing poles and scabrous, rank-smelling Hound Dawgs baying over buckets of pale, moist, wriggling things, from the backs of ancient station wagons or beat-up four-by-fours. Besides, the James River was way up, swollen from the deluge of summer rain, so any lingering hopes he might have had for sinking a line in there were effectively dashed. I should've known better, though.

"Honey," he smiled, contentedly, "Ah'm goin' fishin'."

My own smile was a taut, malevolent slash, as I advanced on him, credit cards in hand. "Oh, no, you're not," I informed him. "The ground is soaked, the river's overflowed its banks, and this isn't New York—all the grocery stores are closed by now ... *and* they don't stock roaches, anyway. Besides, you promised to take me out to the Tobacco Company to eat."

He contemplated the situation for a few seconds. "Well, it's true, Ah promised to do that," he allowed, "an' it's true there ain't an open bait shop or grocery stawh from heah to Wawshin'-tun." He paused, then moved in for the kill. "But it's also true we got a crick about fifteen miles from heah that Ah know for a fact ain't up, an' it's also true we got Vend-o-worm."

My face muscles went numb and my throat dried out. "Vend-o-worm?" I croaked.

"Vend-o-worm," he confirmed. "Come on—we'll take us a little rahhd down to th'corn-nuh stawh."

The store, as I thought, was closed for the night, but outside was a vending machine that I hadn't seen previously. At a glance, it looked like any other automatic munchies dispenser, but inside was a different matter. It gave out *worms*. Long, thin, red ones . . . fat, brown, chunky ones . . . medium-sized gray ones—all in pint-sized plastic bags loaded with water and worm food for a week. They had every kind of worm the average fishing fanatic could possibly crave. This, I know . . . because some depraved Good Ol' Bawh undergoing fly-casting withdrawal had obviously designed and marketed the damn things all across the South.

"I see." I handed him some quarters, and pulled myself up to my full, majestic five-foot-one. "Don't come back without The Big One," I told him, and walked off without a backward glance.

I couldn't understand how desperation could drive a man to buy machine-dispensed worms. What I am still hoping for, though, is the day they all get desperate enough to finally skip the worm bit, and feed machines quarters to spit out the *fish*.

iv. Footbawhl

10 *Of Pigskin and Passion*

It is, perhaps, a little redundant to mention passion and pigskin in the same breath, in relation to Southern Men. After all, Footbawhl is without doubt one of the most hallowed of rituals in the on-going celebration of Southern Manhood. Far holier than Easter to an Orthodox Russian, far more sacrosanct than virginity to a Vestal, is that period of the ecumenical calendar known as Footbawhl Season. We're talking Sacred Pigskin here (or Cowhide, as the case may be).

Southern Men, therefore, take Footbawhl Very Seriously. Writer Paul Hemphill asserts that, down in Alabama, survivors of the '56–'59 Footbawhl seasons can still recall every minute of the game in which the underrecruited Auburn pulled off an eleventh-hour miracle and thrashed their bigger, better-fielded (and less-often suspended) archrivals, Alabama. Nearly thirty years later, you can still see the faded but gloating bumper stickers gracing every moving vehicle—car, four-by-four, mule wagon, or tricycle—in Auburn: "PUNT, 'BAMA, *PUNT*!!"

Memories die hard Down South. So does passion. Prior to their phenomenal win, Auburn residents sported a sign on a downtown telephone pole indicative of both their Conference standing (they'd been slapped on NCAA probation yet again), and their general mood: "Auburn Gives The World 24 Hours To Get The Hell Out Of Town."

Anyway, the point is that to survive the Southern Male, it is essential that you be Very Stoic During Footbawhl (even if you are a fan), or bail out quick. Leave the room, leave the house, leave him—whatever. You might consider a trial separation one autumn. Because, given the choice between His Woman and His

Religion, the Gospel according to St. Howard Cosell will win out every time. There were a slew of male-type vices I had to endure—too many and too foul to mention—in my time with my particular Southern Male; but if I had to choose which of these addictions, obsessions, compulsions, or propensities I'd prefer to deal with, then I would have to opt for an afternoon with the Redneck, the Dawg, an' awhhl th'bawhs. . . .

Footbawhl was the best. I personally loathe the game, but with him, at least it ran the full gamut of human emotion. He lectured, he analyzed, he raged, and he rejoiced, his pulse leaping with each sudden mood change, with each subtle shift of the field. At such times, he was as dangerous as an uncoupled bull moose at the height of mating season. When he was mildly furious, he'd shout, snarl, and spit the most profound, all-encompassing, and sincere epithets an irate Southerner—and only an irate Southerner—is capable of; but when he was really furious, his pupils would shrink to pinpoints, his breathing would become fitful, and he'd take to muttering viciously. The jaw would lock, the eyes would narrow into malevolent slits, and he'd hiss softly to himself:

"You rotten m----------h! You ROTTEN m----------h!"

over and over. Like a litany. When he was ecstatic, he was worse.

Footbawhl was an occupational hazard. For me. I learned to sit up—quick!—every time a really good or really bad play was made, because I ran the risk of having my head slap the leather couch whenever he shot to his feet—and took his lap with him. This maneuver was further complicated by the presence of a somnolent Doberman, whose eighty pounds of sinew invariably landed on me, not the floor, and the free-flying ash from a cigarette now more cinder than butt. The Dallas Cowboys would start to gain ground and he'd explode upward, jubilant, yelling, "Yeahhhh, bu-u-ud-DEEE, YEAHHH!" and send both Dawg and girlfriend bouncing off his chest. I could never decide which was more horrendous: trying to scrape blackened tobacco off of my jeans, or turning slightly to ease a stiff hip—only to come face-to-face with a drooling Dobe. I choose to forget about the ricocheting beers.

There were other dangers, too. I also learned, early on, to gently but firmly remove the Kools from his teeth and tap them clean, before he—no malice intended—forgot and put one out. On me. Little things like that. He taught himself to be careful about that one, though. He'd flick and I'd flinch, alarming the Dawg ("YEEEE-IPPPE!"), thereby necessitating an apology. To the Dawg. "Ah'm sorry," he'd murmur, all tenderness, and give Luke a loving squeeze, and scratch my neck absently ("Goo'bawh . . . goo'bawh . . . "). For months thereafter, I had raging nightmares about him really mixing up his hand signals—kissing the Dawg, and rubbing my ears. Footbawhl was always a trade-off.

The sounds could get pretty unsettling, too. Luke whining,

wheezing, and snuffling through a wet nose, supplicating for attention, against the muffled thud of the other Cowboys fan's heart, and a low, demonic counterpoint of "Hehehhehehehheh-hehHEHHHHH!"'s. Dallas would start to pull ahead and he'd begin to chortle, wickedly, low down inside hi'self: "Hehheheh-hhehehhHEHHHH!" occasionally punctured by a gloating cackle. "Hah-HAH!" he'd bark, "Hahhah-hahhahhahhahhahhah-HAHHH!" savoring every delicious second of the anticipated triumph.

In retrospect, though, he had his crosses to bear. Aside from the combined weight of girlfriend and Doberman on his chest, he had to endure my handing his last cigarette to the Dawg, and giving him a wet Dorito chip in return; or being startled out of the depths of a gripping final quarter by the touch of soft, moist, velvety lips on his ear—and not knowing whose they had been.

Footbawhl. HehhehehhehehhehehehhehHEHHHHHHH...!

11 *Praise the Lawwhhd and Complete the Pass*

A word here about Religion.

There are but two religions practiced Down South, the first of which is Protestantism (in its various forms).

The second, as I said, is Footbawhl.

Most Protestant denominations require baptism for admittance into the Church. Footbawhl just requires a Y chromosome.

Oh, sure, you could point out—correctly—that there are Catholics in Louisiana, and more than a few Jews scattered throughout Dixie, but so what? The South is the Bible Belt of the nation, and the Bible down there is King Jay-yems.

However, the Good Lawwhhd wanted the South to have Footbawhl as well as The Word. In fact, He wanted Dixie to have the Almighty Protestant Pigskin so badly, He even let the game be played by Blacks, Catholics, Cajuns, Creoles, Sabines, "Hunkies," Socialists, and other indigenous Foreign Elements, because when it comes to Footbawhl there's no such thing as religious or ethnic differences. Or the Sabbath.

And so, on the seventh day, Gawd made Footbawhl. And it was good. Because with Footbawhl came scholarships, and with scholarships came educations, and with educations came careers, and with careers came money, whether a son of the South made it to the big time or not. Of course, if he did, he made even more money than the average college graduate, got famous, and enhanced Dixie's well-earned reputation as a nursery for future NFL superstars. And it made the man's school very happy, and his coach very happy, and His Mama and Dai-dy very happy, and his agent *very*, very happy. And gave the minister and everyone else in the local church the following Sunday something to thank Gawd and praise Jesus for. It satisfied numerous considerations—economic, scholastic, religious, and regional pride—in one glorious, full-blown shot.

This is why Footbawhl and Religion are virtually synonymous below the Mason-Dixon line. There, Footbawhl, like church, is the celebration of community, a ritual proclamation that Our People Are Here, and They Are Prevailing. Both are a rallying point for common blood, common beliefs, and common history. Amen. But they are also focal points of regional culture, instruments of psychic survival and, as such, are strong advertising for the twentieth-century version of *le beau sabreur*, of all that is Good and Mighty and Just in the world. There's nothing like having a squad of 260-pound Protestant Warriors with coiled-spring throwing arms to make a solid case for doing your praying in public.

At any rate, I got an almost immediate introduction to this logic in—strangely enough—church. He was a devout agnostic, but His Mama was a Believer of the first magnitude. So half of the clan went to the service. The other half watched it on TV.

Her first error, I guess, was taking a Catholic-reared atheist to an Episcopalian church. Things went smoothly enough in the beginning, to our credit; after a while, though, comes a point in the service known as the invocation. I was prepared for supplications unto the Lord for ending world hunger, for peace on earth—maybe even for a Republican landslide on November 4—but not for the Almighty's blessing on the upcoming UVA-VPI game.

"Please, oh, Lawwhhd," intoned their priest, "we *need* this one!"

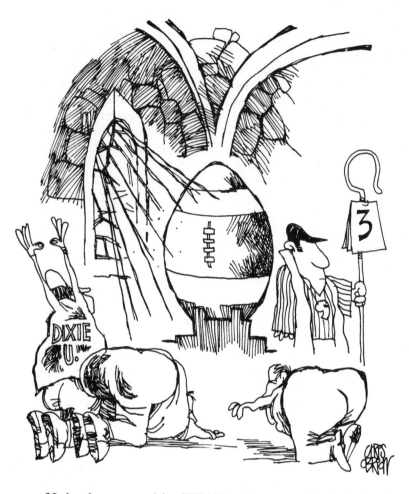

My head came up with a WHAP! as the neurons in the back of my brain overloaded and fried out. *Praying for Footbawhl*? For a game involving a piece of pig and a bunch of men in funny zebra shirts? For a horde of knuckle-dragging behemoths, thundering across the Virginia veldts? *Footbawhl*?

Yes. Footbawhl. The priest cleared his throat and turned solemn, bloodhound eyes heavenward. "Let us pray," he breathed.

And they did.

And there is nothing like the power of high-voltage Protestant prayer, with a kickoff less than an hour away, for putting The Fix in. The adrenalin supply boils up into the brain, the nerves burn raw, like ulcers shot full of battery acid, and the average, mild-mannered parish pastor turns into a thunder-eyed, fire-eating, latter-day Prophet. I had, of course, heard countless clergymen use David's triumph over Goliath as a metaphor for Good overcoming Evil, but never when the Forces Of Darkness in question were a handful of young, jersey-clad Virginian males who, even as we prayed, were preparing to wage war against an equally youthful brigade of Christian Soldiers. But then again, I'd never seen a group of Episcopalians devolve into a rabid seethe of Baptists, either—like this one just had.

"'And WOO-O-O-OE,' sayeth th'Lawwhhd," the priest thundered, "'WO-O-OOE unto him who would come into our midst, an' destroy that which is Good, that which is Holy! For Ah say unto you, th'Ahmmies of th'Awhmahh-ty will smahht he who cometh in See-yin'—smahht him to th' ground, Ah tell you!— 'an' Truth an' Honnuh an' Rahhteousnuss shall prevail!'"

Well . . . hey . . . say hallelujah, brother. I could see his brethren in Pigskin getting religion in a major way. They weren't moaning and swaying, exactly, but there was a certain eyeball-numbed ecstasy seeping through their ranks, a certain tongue-drying hoarseness in the way they mumbled their prayers and turned their moistened, hopeful faces Deity-ward. Only Southern Protestants can pull this off. Their Puritan co-religionists to the North, while burning with the same hell-fire zeal, the same ferret-eyed ferocity, usually maintain a measure of restraint in their worship, a certain respectful distance from their Creator, as do the Episcopalians themselves—usually. But with Southerners, as I've pointed out, everything is personal. So it was with this familiarity, born of the knowledge that Protestants in general—and Virginians in particular—sit at the right hand of God, that the parish of St. Luke's thus addressed the Almighty:

"Lawwhhd, y'all know you owe us this one!"

That about did it for me. I now knew that if these folks lost this game they'd be intolerable next week, and if they won they'd be even more intolerable. It was therefore with a sense of both futility and trepidation that I followed the throng down to the stadium, telling myself that if, indeed, God did exist, there would be a rain-out . . . a draw . . . a cloud of locusts, perhaps . . . anything that would delay this battle of the heavens until I was safely out of town.

It was not to be. Any Footbawhl game in the South can be played in the midst of Armageddon, if necessary—which is, in a sense, what it is. Southern Footbawhl teams are generously stocked with free-living, rough-playing young men who hit hard and hate long, thereby satisfying the bloodlust of their families, friends, and the other reasonably innocent bystanders packing the bleachers. It's a very serious business, in which both squads take the week between games to plot revenge, assuage bruised egos, and hate the other side a lot; so a little thing like the elements, divine intervention, or full-scale nuclear war isn't about to stop them.

Anyway, the game was played, and it and the next few days passed in a merciful blur for me. Needless to say, the Lord had seen fit to smile upon the parish of St. Luke's, so, come Sunday, the congregation was especially jubilant and God-fearing—and smug. But they controlled it well. No out-and-out mention was made of the Almighty's having demonstrated their Election; but suddenly, I met His Mama's black eyes crackling at me over her missal.

"Well," she cooed, "It's almost enough to make an Episcopalian out'a you, ain't it?"

I glanced up in mid-prayer and smiled back at her, totally guileless. "It would be, except for one thing—"

She bent over and followed my finger, tracing the text of the credo:

". . . I believe in the one, the true, the everlasting, *catholic* church—"

And damn near brained me, still smirking, with her Bible.

It didn't end there. Months later I picked up an anthology of Southern memoirs and winced when I read the recollections of one Texan brought up in the Depression. He wrote that ". . . a float of paper flowers said it best, in the Spring Roundup Parade on the campus in 1938 . . . it had a Bible made of black paper flowers and a brown flower football and a student standing between them in a football uniform. On the side of the float were the words: 'The Answer To Our Prayers.' "

That, in itself, was enough for me, but "the answer," he went on to write, was the school's new football coach, a Legend In His Own Time.

And the coach's name?

Dana X. Bible.

Onward, Christian Soldiers!

v. Hound Dawgs

12 Nevvuh Come Between a May-yan an' his Hound Dawg

It was his father who pointed out that I made a grievous error in relating the afternoon of Footbawhl with his son and the Dawg.

"No Southern bawh," he told me, "would evvuh bounce His Dawg to th'flawwh." Pause. "His Woman, sure, but"—(horrified gasp)—"*not His Dawg!*"

He was, of course, right.

After all, y'all can hunt with a Dawg.

Y'all can go drinkin' with a Dawg.

And, yes, you can even sleep with one, too (in the literal sense), a fact I had driven home to me the hard way. So who needs the Woman? Once I had the importance of the all-purpose Dawg seared, forever, into the gray folds of my brain, I felt compelled to amend the following truths—

(1) Girlfriend—very like ashtray.

(2) Girlfriend—very like Hound Dawg.

—in fairness to the *Dawg*.

Because the Dawg, to the Southern Male, is an essential and eminently portable entity. Practical considerations aside, the Dawg is the Southern Man's living link with his frontier/backwoods/farming/hunting roots; a vital *ipso facto* symbol of virile masculinity, a constant massage to his ego, and a four-legged embodiment of his personal connection with the wildlife and natural history of his region. Southerners—by circumstance, and probably choice, too—are natural ecologists: masters of all they survey, lovers of the land they sprung from. Ergo, the Dawg is

I.D. and Heritage. The Dawg is Paramount. The Dawg is Cherished. The Dawg is One Of The Bawhs.

And the Dawg always understands him when His Woman don't.

That's why the Dawg is so portable. He goes where no self-respecting Southerner would ever take His Woman: to poker games and bar-hopping with the bawhs, fishing, hunting, for lazy lopes along the beach, or for three hours' worth of Footbawhl-watching. The woman could be a natural athlete, a natural alcoholic, and possess the razor-sharp instincts and idiotic élan of a moonshine runner—but she'll still sit at home. The Dawg, however, goes everywhere. It stays put, shuts up, and comes when It's called, which is, I suppose, more than a Southern Male can say about any self-respecting woman (His or anyone else's). The Dawg, in short, travels in trust.

However, I never realized how deep the feeling between Southern Men and Dawgs ran, until the day I helped load equipment and provisions into the depths of his new boat. His eyes glittering gleefully, he carefully pointed out each and every feature of his new plaything, ran his hands over her sleek teak paneling, and patted her velour berths. It was love. The euphoria lasted until he began investigating the emergency equipment and supplies: the self-inflating life raft, the fishing lines, compasses, maps, food, tide tables.

"But where are the life jackets?" I asked.

He paused, rummaged briefly, and pulled out one lone jacket. A shrunken and oddly-shaped little jacket.

"Whose is *that*?"

His eyes bulged incredulously. *"Luke's!"* he barked, stunned, "who else's?" He shook his head slowly, throwing me a furtive glance as he backed off in wary disbelief.

"What about us? You? Guests? *Me*?"

He considered the problem briefly.

"You," he announced, "can swim othuh strokes than the dawggie paddle."

"I swear to God," I hissed, "you think more of the damn dog than you do of me!"

He took a philosophical drag of his cigarette. "We-ee-ell," he reasoned, "Ah can get $2,000 for the Dawg, an' about *zippo* for *you.* . . . "

Steamroller logic. But it didn't prevent me from bouncing a

frying pan off his head. I dropped the subject forever—however, I also kept digging till I found the other jackets.

Having lost that round so conclusively to the Dawg, you'd think I'd put up, shut up, and mind my new place in the Pork Chop Hierarchy. But those stubborn, dangerous, reactionary Yankee misconceptions had a nasty way of resurfacing around him, so I found myself, yet again, butting snouts with Dawg and Good Ol' Bawh alike.

It came down to the berth. It was in his wilder, halcyon, "bachelor" days, before the new boat, that he used to share his percale-clad prow and his cheeseburgers with his Dawg and Buddy, draped sleepily along the long throw of his legs as they conferred on the correct point-spread for the Cowboys. As long as the game was on, I had no problem restricting myself to occasionally taking a pulse or throwing a Dorito chip to one or the other or both (hard to tell, sometimes); but as night fell, my ugly, lunatic, suicidal Northern Female personality defects reasserted themselves—especially when confronted with the new satin sheets.

"Come to bed, love," he invited, with his best Rhett Butleresque half-smile. Ears and all.

I nailed the Dawg with an icy stare.

"What's the matter?," he asked.

"The Dawg," I hissed.

He looked blank. "Y'all don't lahhk th'Dawg?"

"I like the Dawg fine," I replied, "as a person. He's a good guy—really—but I don't especially want to *sleep* with him."

His eyes flattened into evil, reptilian slits. Luke looked forlorn.

"The Dawg," he muttered nastily, "*always* sleeps with me."

"The Dawg," I retorted, "is out of luck."

He wrenched his pupils from my face in disgust, as the same primordial instinct buried deep in Luke's brain or nerve endings or canine gut told him, without doubt, that he was going to lose this one. He batted long Doberman lashes at his master, and with a final plaintive whine and a quick flip of his tongue on my hand, made as if to drag his drooping haunches away. Into the night.

His fellow Cowboys fan looked bereaved. "Ah'm sorry, buddy," he mourned, "y'all a good guy." He rubbed Luke's ears and sighed. "Ah love you—you know that." Luke sighed back, shrugged, and gently wheezed through wet, leathery nostrils. *Women*, he said.

"She's okay," his Dai-dy explained, "she jus' doan know any

bettuh." Luke wheezed again and shuffled off to the other berth. He understood. I probably would have, too, if I at least had my ears rubbed occasionally. . . .

But no. Even in exile, the Dawg still exercised a pervasive influence. His human doppelgänger leaned across me suddenly as we settled into bed, a hand wrapped round my back, the other buried in my hair. He radiated tenderness, affection, and a relentless concern.

"Y'awwhrahht?" he whispered.

I smiled up at him in the darkness. "Mmmm-hmmm . . . " I purred.

He whipped on the light, eyebrows arched in alarm. "*Are* you?" Before I could answer, the Dawg whined back—low, soulful, heart-rending: "H-hhh-h-nnhh . . . "

"Goo'bawh," he murmured, reassured, "Y'all a goo-bawh . . . " He hestitated fractionally, then glanced at me. "How 'bout you?"

I snapped the light off in a fury. "Good *night*!" I spat back.

I could hear him rasp a hot sigh and see his eyes roll skullward, as he shook his fist up at the sky and asked the age-old question: "Now what did Ah do wrong?"

And silently answer himself: Women! *Yankee* women!

If you can't beat 'em, join 'em. I took a cue from the Dawg and slithered my way up his side—slowly, sneakily—until I'd tunneled about eighty pounds of myself onto his chest and left leg. He stirred drowsily.

"Heyyy, bud-DEE," he rumbled, eyes closed in bliss, "How yuh doin'?"

I said nothing, just continued to breathe—and wait. Big hug. I felt a few of my smaller ribs go—SNAAPP!

"You're so good," he went on. "Y'listen to me, y'put up with me, keep me cump-ny day an' nahht—you're a good person, y'-know?"

"Ah know," I drawled back.

His eyes flew open, spinning like searchlights. I could see the shock freeze on his face, see his mouth twitch uncontrollably as he absorbed the total impact of his discovery. Nearly a full minute went by before he found words.

"We-e-ell," he slowly conceded, "you ain't so bad yowh'sel'." He shifted his weight a little, rubbed my ear, and tentatively patted me on the back.

"'Fact," he ventured, "you're ev'ry bit as good as him." He gave my side two resounding thumps, chuckled, and sighed contentedly.

"That's what Ah reckoned," I drawled.

"Oh—whah's that?"

I smiled my best, tight, Jack Nicholson killer-alligator smile at him, and went for the throat. "Girlfriend," I told him, "very lahhhk Hound Dawg."

And slipped into sleep on his raging.

13 *The One with the Waggedy Tail*

Hound dawgs, I learned, were a volatile issue. New York being the home of the Westminster Dog Show, the city is lavishly stocked with canines of every description and pedigree—usually a little heavier on the first consideration than the second. One would think, then, that New Yorkers would be the nation's experts on all things canine, considering they spend more time showing their hounds, searching for safe places to walk them, and nimbly sidestepping their pets' most prolific contribution to day-to-day living, than most other Americans. After all, it was the denizens of the Big Apple who flocked to the sidewalks with their designer doggy scoops from Bloomingdale's, rather than get penalized under the "pooper scooper" law—or be forced to give up their dogs entirely; and it is those same folks who know exactly how many dogs—and of what size, temperament and breed—can reasonably be added to the surroundings, before the noise or smell or general proximity of still *more* warm, breathing bodies packed into a building finally turn their neighbors into dog-hating homicidal maniacs. New Yorkers, then, both have an affection for dogs, and could safely be considered experts in their care, feeding, and adapting them to the rigors of their environment.

Not so. Forget the breeders, the judges, and the veterinarians. Forget the natural scientists and the evolutionists. Forget even the lifelong dog-lover; the only genuine canine expert in the United States—if not the world—is the Southern Man in your life.

The Northern Woman knows this already. She has already been told—several times—that her Man has the best eye in the Chitlin Belt for picking and training bird-, coon-, or general all-purpose Dawgs; she has already heard about his amazing Dawg Blaze, who would actually climb trees—*grown trees!*—to tackle the fiercest bobcat in the South; and she has already been given chapter and verse on Uncle Joe's Spike, the best tracking dawg ever to terrorize the bootleggers of Lincoln county. What she doesn't know, however, is that the actual choice of Dawg is a highly personal and sensitive one for her Man, and if she wishes to remain a viable element in her relationship with him, she won't even broach the subject. *Ever.*

We were in the middle of an open-air party at a coworker's baronial spread in New Jersey, when the office's entire Southern contingent slowly began to congregate around the beer kegs. I began—rather wisely, I thought—to edge away towards the safety of the swimming pool, but a firm, strong hand grabbed mine, and began dragging me headlong into their midst.

"It's awwh-rahht," my Southern Male explained, "it's just a bunch of Good Ol' Bawhs shootin' the breeze."

"That isn't what worries me," I told him. "What worries me is they're shooting the breeze about dogs."

His eyebrows rippled upward happily. "Dawgs, huh?" he mused. "Should be interestin'."

"Should be dangerous, you mean. The last time you got into a discussion on dogs, you nearly got stitches in your head, and I came close to swimming home from the Great South Bay. Why don't we stick to something safe and soothing—like wrestling on TV, or U.S. aid to the contras or something?"

"Naww, nawww, you're over-reacting," he assured me. "Everything'll be just fahhn."

And it was. Until our host's Irish setter came bounding into the proceedings, tail swishing, tongue flapping, and his red coat gleaming in the sunshine. He was a gorgeous, friendly, intelligent soul—and Stanley made the mistake of saying so.

A half-dozen pairs of eyes immediately ground Stanley to powdered glass. Seconds ticked by, slowly and heavily, until George finally pushed up his glasses and spoke for the group.

"Yeahh, Harry's an awhhl-rahht kahhnd of person," he carefully intoned, "fo' a *designer* dawg."

Stanley's head snapped up violently. I could see his eyes bulge as his temples thundered with blood, and his tongue dried out. George had clearly hit him right where he lived.

"A . . . a what?" he quavered.

The Bawhs rolled their eyes up in exasperation and sighed into their beers.

"A designer dawg," explained George, "instead of a *real* one."

"What the hell are you talking about?" screamed Stanley. "Harry's got the best bloodlines in the States! His sire was five times a Grand Champion! His mother's produced three regional champions already! What do you mean, 'a real dog'? Just what are you saying is *wrong* with Harry?"

Dennis spoke up this time, regarding his friend with infinite, patient compassion. "Stanley," he said, ever so soothingly, "does Harry hunt?"

Stanley shook his head.

"At *all*?"

Stanley studied the toe of his boots and shrugged.

"*Anything*?"

Stanley shook his head a final time, and sighed to himself. "No," he whispered, "he's a pet."

Dennis winced and bit his cigarette in half. The rest of the Bawhs just shuddered.

"The dawg's a gawddamn Irish settuh!" Dennis spat, "don't he even *set*?"

Harry's master's eyes fluttered weakly upward for a moment. "No," he croaked, "he's just *ours*."

The porkchop prophets stirred, and began muttering darkly. Truly, there was menace in the air, but Dennis quelled it and made a one last effort to salvage the situation.

"Stanley," he breathed, "just what *do* you do with Harry?"

Six pairs of sleepy Southern eyes rolled soulfully in their sockets; six pairs of eyes implored him to come up with something—anything—that would justify Stanley throwing away a few thousand dollars on a useless dog; six pairs of eyes locked on him with laser-beam intensity, waiting for him to think of the one acceptable thing that would allow a grown man to be seen, *in public*, with such a sorry excuse of a Dawg as Harry.

Stanley cleared his throat, and met Dennis's eye. "Well," he rasped, brokenly, "we look at him."

A hideous groan ripped through the air, as the Bawhs staggered wildly, blindly, insane with disgust, and flung their beers to the ground. *Only in New York*, I heard them think, would an adult male buy a Dawg to *look* at.

It was George who finally took pity on his host. "Y'don't undduhstahhn', sportsfan," he began. "It's just that...down South, we use our dawgs, an' we take 'em as they come—halfwolf, half-shark, we don't care—"

"Long as they can hunt, guard the house, an' round up lahhvstawhk occasionally," said Dennis.

"Rahhht," added a buddy, "an' can set still whahl we watch Footbawhl or play poker."

"Hell, mongrels're better to hunt with, anyhow," opined George. "They're robust, they got the best traits of more than one breed, they ain't too hahh-strung, and they're usually good people. You can trust 'em 'round the kids, fo' a start." He peered at Harry, grimacing sourly. "An' we don't have to mortgage the place off to own one!"

Stanley flinched fractionally, but wisely kept quiet. Dennis, however, caught his involuntary movement.

"By the way," he drawled, "how much did you pay for ol' Harry, anyway?"

His victim stared at him bleakly. "Enough," he rasped. Dennis gave him a leery squint. "I don't remember," Stanley blurted, "it's on my American Express!"

Hysterical guffaws erupted from the throng. About four of them collapsed on the ground, helpless with laughter, their fried chicken flung crazily into the air as they writhed uncontrollably on the lawn. I sensed that, given the state of his comrades, Stanley was at least safe from lynching, tar-and-feathering, or being run out of town, but this was of small comfort to him. His reputation was in shreds, his taste and judgment had been mangled, and there were at least ten pounds of food defiling his tulip beds. I couldn't help but feel bad for the guy. Not so my Southern Man. He lay on the grass with the rest of the gasping, twitching humps, waited for them to catch their breaths, and unerringly chose his moment.

"Dahhhm," he cracked, "Stanley's just bought his'sel' a Gucci Poochy!" More hysteria. Dennis cried on George, who clung to a chair. Allan lurched into Charlie, who emptied a Michelob on his head, and Ray and Bill flailed around in the dirt while Harry just sniffed at the thrashing men, and eyed his master questioningly.

"Hell," one of them ventured, "I'd rather hunt in pantyhose!"

Something within Stanley snapped at that moment. Striding among the prone bodies, he began booting them until, weak and reeling with exhaustion, all the members of the Fatback Fraternity were firmly back on their feet.

"Now you listen up!" Stanley snarled. "I paid good money for that dog! He's a purebred, he's a champion, and he's just as good as any dog you put him up against. You think you can do it, you guys whip him into shape and make a hunting dog outta him, if you're so smart!"

A handful of Frat brothers began to snicker quietly. "No chance," said Ray, "th'dawg just don't have it."

"Have what?"

"The blood," answered one.

"The concentration," answered another.

"The *sense*," said George.

Stanley regarded Harry sorrowfully. "Don't feel bad," said Dennis. "You bought him because he was beautiful, he was gentle, he was affectionate, and he was smart. He was never supposed to be a working dawg. He's just a friend. That's a good enough reason to have him." He paused, and softly tugged Harry's silky ears. "To tell you the truth, that's why most of us grew up with dawgs. To keep us comp'ny whahl we hunted or fished or camped. It's a real personal kahhnd of thing, Stan, so if Harry is what you want . . . well, enjoy him."

"Well, now, Ah don't know," mused George. "Harry's a settuh, an' they're bird dawgs. He don't *have* to have hound blood or mixed blood to be a good dawg, so maybe we can save him, yet." Harry flopped, belly-up, on the grass, and lolled his tongue at George happily. "Then again," he reconsidered, "maybe not." He stooped to scratch the dog's stomach, cleaned off his glasses, and sighed. Harry just slobbered at him. "Stanley," George stated, "looks like you're just gonna have to whip out that ol' AmEx card of yours and get yoursel' a real Dawg, after all."

A fierce mote of desperation glinted in Stanley's eyes, as he seized George by the sleeve. "Tell me," he begged him, "tell me what kind!"

George looked at Dennis who looked at Ray, who shot a covert glance at my smirking Southern Man. "We-e-elll," he drawled, "seems you're gonna need sumthin' rare. Sumthin' special. Sumthin' you can show off to your Westminstuh friends with pride. Sumthin' nobody else in New York can *evvuh claim to have*." He grinned at George, who buried his face into his beer. "And Ah can get you one from Louisiana for . . . oooohh . . . only about five thousand dollars or so. Best huntin', cow-, or hawg-dawg in the South."

Stanley nearly ripped the check he was writing in his haste to hand it over.

"Fine, fine, just fine," he stammered, "just tell what kind it is."

A smile sliced the face of my Southern soulmate as he pocketed the check, took Stanley by the hand, and shook it warmly. "Good buddy," he told him, "you now own a genuine Catahoula Leopard Dawg."

"Like hell I do!" Stanley shouted. "There's no such animal!" He hesitated fractionally. "Is there?"

George grinned teeth from here to Tupelo. "'Fraid so," he pointed out. "In fact, it's the state dog of Louisiana. Pretty good dawgs, too—providing you kin catch 'em—"

"—an' tame 'em," interjected Dennis.

"—an' know where to look fo' 'em," he finished. "'Course, they're all ovvuh th'place, so you just bought yoursel' the most expensive Leopard Dawg in the continental U.S.!"

Stanley stared morosely at his scorched checkbook. The last thing I recall, with any clarity, was the sight of George and Dennis, creased over in fits, collapsing onto my beloved and taking the rest of the Frat brothers down with them. I can still see Harry look quizzically at his master, waiting for someone to explain it all to him. And I can see Stanley—still waiting, too.

vi. Food

14 Grits—The Final Frontier

First of all, there are Southern women who don't like grits. However, these women either:

(1) control the family purse-strings;
(2) changed their names;
(3) moved North;
(4) changed their names and moved North; or
(5) have been excommunicated from their respective churches.

A Northern woman in love with a Southern man has no such options. 'Round 'bout 1866, the denizens of the South finally realized that the Confederacy would, come hell or high water, be cleaved unto the Union—forcibly, bloodily, but inevitably. And equally inevitably would come the day that some fool Southerner—male or female—would cast both reason and good name to the winds, and up and marry a Nawwthen'uh. Worse, still, is that hybrids from those unions would result—hybrids neither Northern nor Southern. Hybrids more dangerous and . . . well . . . just *tackier* than any purebred Yankee because they could pass for Southern; hybrids who could, with the slow seepage of time and the steady dilution of Southern blood, unravel the very fabric of Dixie culture, society and—let's face it—psycho-history.

And so the South made grits. And they were good—in a socio-political/mythological sense. Because grits are what separated the sheep from the goats. You either had to be a Southerner born or bred to tolerate them, or so willing to "convert" that you would martyr yourself in the face of an onslaught of grits, chitlins, moonshine, and other gastronomic outrages. Survival didn't

make you a Southerner, understand—it only may have made you
marginally acceptable as one. You had to be pretty serious about
turning Southward before crossing the Grits Frontier.

But what if you were a Yankee who actually *liked* grits? Well,
before the homogenization of America (Southern) with America
(Northern) resulted in the South (New), there were always several other lines of demarcation. It was either bluegrass, C&W,
tobacco-chewing, or some other Southern art form. Or hunting,
fishing, dancin'-an'-fightin' (Southern Male), or Home-cookin',
cannin', picklin', an' bakin' (Southern Female). And Eyelash
Battin' (Southern Belle). By the time you were able to hold your
own at any combination of these art forms assigned to your gen-
der, you had given up so much of your original identity, that ethnic and/or geographical background ceased to matter—you were
a Goner.

Hence grits are a Big Deal. Aside from the fact that millions of Southerners have been weaned on the stuff and love it to death anyway, they have historical, social, and cultural ramifications a lot more far-reaching than any bowl of Quaker Oats ever did. They are as much a symbol of ethnic identification to the South as kim-chi is to Korea (and are about as delectable, too).

But having a knowledge of grits (beyond: 1., gravel, and 2., chutzpah) won't do. Finding out just what grits are is easy enough; finding out what you do with them, however, requires serious steepage in what has evolved into a closely-protected and highly esoteric priesthood. Here is where a Yankee starts losing ground, because here is where Southern Women uncharacteristically clam up about housewifely arts. You ain't fit to be a Southern Man's woman unless you fix grits on your own steam, and the natives sure as hell ain't about to tell you. Y'all have to earn that knowledge and work your own way out of the leper colony.

I knew I was "in" the day His Mama and His Nanny set to rectify the gaping holes in my education. Living, as he did, in my hometown of New Yawwhhk, they no doubt feared I was both starving him on damyankee food, and letting a slice of culinary heritage die off with him. Or maybe they just bled for the poah' chile whose Mama had been tacky enough to overlook certain vital aspects of her upbringing—Lawwhhd'a'muhcy! I had thought I was ahead of the game: I knew what grits were, I knew how to fix Basic Grits, and I knew they were served only for breakfast. That's all I knew.

"Su-guh," I was told, "you doan know *diddly-squat.*"

Oh.

They had a point. There's things that you do to grits. Boiled grits. Fried grits. Garlic n' cheese grits. Buttered and salted grits. Itsy bitsy grits. By the end of the morning, I had had it Up to There in grits.

"Enough!" I surrendered. "I doubt the boy's eaten that many kinds of grits in his life. There's nothing more you can do to grits that you ladies haven't done already!"

"Ah-hahhhh!" gloated His Mama. She stabbed me with a bright eye, dug around her stores, and triumphantly produced an anonymous tin can. "Y'all obviously ovvuhlooked the Fish Roe Factor."

Oh, God, *fish roe.* Trust the goddamn Southerners to come up with some off-beat food from way out of left field, and then dish it up for breakfast. I examined the can queasily, as they examined my face.

"What's the mattuh?" one asked. I grimaced. They grinned happily, enjoying every minute of my discomfort. "Jus' think of it as Southern caviar."

Oh, no, no, no . . . not that. That was like calling chopped liver Jewish paté. That's like calling a Hershey Kiss a chocolate-amaretto truffle. Oh, no. No way.

His Mama smiled beatifically and shook the goo from the can. It fell with a wet plop—schhllupp-uppp!—glistening pale, moist, and congealed. It made me think of a school of dead whales, of soft white underbellies blubber-up under an anemic gray sky. . . . Ugggghhhhh.

"Put it ba-a-ackk!" I pleaded.

His Nanny grinned this time, her smile as wide as a watermelon rind, as her daughter advanced on the roe with a wooden spoon. She began mashing it with a fine, haughty, Lady Mac-Beth-like disdain, with a deliberate, maniacal intensity that was chilling in its thoroughness. WHAP! she went, whap!-whap!-whap!-grin-whap!whap!-grin, grin-whap!-gri-i-inn,-WHAP! and flipped it into the skillet with a ruthless flick.

"Needs th'milk, Ah reckon," she told her mother. Nanny grunted shortly.

"Milk?" I gagged.

"Oh, Lawwhhdawh'mahhty, ye-easss!" they both chimed, in unison. In went the milk with a hot hiss.

By now the combined effluvium of grits and roe had completely overcome my delicate Northern sensibilities. I groped blindly for the door, the tears scalding me. I could hear the womenfolk cackling over their cauldrons as I staggered out into the morning light. His Mama, as usual, had the final word:

"Sure y'all doan wanna help gut the hawg foah' Chitlin Nahhht?"

Grits followed me home. Just when I thought I'd heard the last of them, an editor I work with fixed a baleful blue eye on me, put my manuscript down and said, "You doan know whut you're missin' with gree-yits." (Pronounced correctly, with two syllables.)

Allow me to elucidate. This man is usually a charming, intelligent, highly articulate S'u'nn Gennelmin, his urbane gloss a lovely counterpoint to his even lovelier down-home Mississippi roots. But that cosmopolitan smoothness cracks dangerously every tahhm he gits t'tawwhhkin' 'bout Home or anythin' related to Home, and the subject of Home Cookin' just about undoes him completely. Grits, therefore, was a highly important and personal topic for him.

I listened to him very carefully. Listened to him rhapsodize about Grits in their various forms, Grits as epicurean Nirvana, Grits in History, and Grits as Savior of the Nation, and eventually, I began to grit my teeth in exasperation. I only wanted to know one thing about grits—one thing, that would close the whole discussion for me. Finally and forever.

"Okay, you grit-grinding omnivore," I snapped, "you love 'em so much, just tell me this—"

"What?" he prompted. I leaned forward, and pounced.

"Grits," I sneered, "singular or plural?"

George's face imploded. I watched this well-read, well-informed, walking Brain Trust chew on the problem for a full five minutes. The answer came, but it sure came slowly.

"Gree-yits," he intoned carefully, "... is ... uh ... *Gree-yits.*"

Precisely. Authentically. With *both* syllables. Sho' nuff are some lines of separation remaining.

And that, as far as I was concerned, answered a number of questions.

But not all of them. There have been, God knows, numerous little conflicts between the North and South over the years—industrial rivalry, cultural clashes, and that small misunderstanding back in the 1860's—but I never fully appreciated how deep the chasm between Yankee and Rebel epicurean sensibilities was, until the subject of barbecue came up. Not even grits had ignited such a sulphurous, brain-inflaming controversy.

It began innocently enough, as most things concerning Southerners do. Dennis and I were discussing grits, and halfway betwen chitlins and fish roe, he suddenly winced and gnashed his teeth.

"Trouble is, you Northerners just don't understand Southern food. You folks don't even know what barbecue is."

Whoa. Now wait a minute. New York–born though I was, I still had family with roots in Texas, Louisiana, and (indirectly) Virginia and the Carolinas, and I was pretty sure I knew good barbecue when I saw it. You don't tell a New Yorker—who, by definition, spends the better part of his or her life eating—that she doesn't know her food. Not unless you wish to leave New York. Immediately.

"No, no, no, you don't! Y'see, you guys do sissy stuff like cover it in . . . in . . . spaghetti sauce and such. I'm talking *real* barbecue."

Uh-huh. A picture was forming in my mind of possum, armadillo, and roadkill grilled over hickory—how "real" can you get, after all? But I held my tongue.

And that was my first mistake. Because, as I've illustrated, when you take to discussing Home Cookin' with Southerners, they lose in a blinding flash whatever Yankee veneer they've acquired Up Nawwhhth. They could be standing there in $150 Gucci loafers, a Ralph Lauren sports jacket, and a Brooks Brothers polo shirt, but biology will always win out: their eyes defocus wistfully, they hook their fingers in their belt-loops or back pockets, and their native Drawhls begin to unfurl . . . slowly, softly, melodically . . . until their vowels are longer than the Alaska Pipe-Lahhn. You can almost smell that Southern soul food wafting on the breeze. . . .

And it always attracts other Southerners, until you have a gaggle of Good Ol' Bawhs around the water cooler, debating the merits of various Footbawhl teams, Dawgs, Booze, and Wimmen (in that order), with one beleaguered Yankee trapped in the middle.

It turned out that Dennis and George, of grits fame, had been busy over the past year. The good Lord saw fit to have them earn their livings amongst Yankees (which was okay, they supposed), but the drawback to this was that He transplanted them light-years away from Real Barbecue. So George and Dennis began looking. They sought out—in the wilds of New Jersey, in the opulent ethnic mix of New York, in the redneck hamlets of eastern Long Island—the one, the true, the only joint that could produce Real Barbecue. It was a quest for Truth. It was the pursuit of Perfection. It was the Holy Grail Over An Open Pit.

And it wasn't easy. As the Great Let's-Cook-It-Over-Mesquite-Craze infected New York, George and Dennis saw their hopes raised and dashed a million times. Oh, sure, there were many fine Southern-style restaurants in the city—but not one of these, the boys informed me, could serve up real Real Barbecue. And they began making me crazy with it:

"How 'bout this, George?"

"Nuh-uhh."

"Why not?"

Pause. "It's just not . . . *real*."

Or:

"Hey, Dennis, you ever try—"

"Uh-huh."

"How did you know what I was going to ask?"

"Does it come outta New York, New Jersey, Connecticut, or Pennsylvania?"

"Uhhhhh . . . yeahhh. . . . "

"I've tried it."

"And?"

And a mournful Dennis would look at an equally morose George and sigh, "It's just not Real."

The situation was approaching critical. Here it was, on the edge of summer, and the boys were still without a Real Barbecue joint. I began to fear for them. Their EKGs were still registering some blips, but both were starting to drag around the newsroom like hungover bloodhounds. Truly, some drastic action was called for.

"Hey-a, Dennis," I finally demanded, "just what constitutes Real Barbecue?" Dennis peeled lifeless eyes off of his computer screen.

"Real?" he croaked, brokenly. I nodded.

A brittle smile cracked his haggard face. The memories of glorious days gone by began to trickle back. I could see him starting to find his rhythm again, starting to exult, once more, in the pure, DNA-deep joy of pit-cooked food, the olfactory ecstasy brought back into sharp focus simply by his recalling the mechanics of roasting meat . . . aaaahhhhhhhh!

"Well, first thing about barbecue," he murmured, "is . . . it's gotta come in pints."

George came over and the two hunkered down and hunched forward, grins as wide as the Mississippi. They were obviously savoring this.

"Second," George whispered back, "is . . . it cay-yant be red." The Bawhs shuddered in spite of themselves, and took quick, panicked drags of their cigarettes.

"Third," Dennis hissed, with a cautionary glance around, "an' most importantly, Ah feel—"

"Oh, absolutely," agreed George, as they both scrunched forward, a scant eyeball away, to deliver their final arcane truism:

"It cay-yant evvuh be identifah-ible!"

The words ricocheted around the room. Typewriters and telephones stopped. The Bawhs slowly pulled themselves back into their seats, all the while eyeing their colleagues with cold distrust. The room resumed its tempo. It was a long time, however, before any of us spoke.

"That's *it*?" I rasped, nasty, "those are your total accumulated thoughts on Real Barbecue? That it be dead, not red, and of dubious origins? This is what you've been pining for all this time? Oh, come on, guys!" The Barbecue Brothers chuckled indulgently. Heh-heh-heh-heh-heh! George wiped a tear from under his glasses. Dennis just shook his head. Heh-heh-heh-heh!

"You don't undduh-stahhhn'," he explained, "that's the beauty of it all. All this time, these Yankees're thinking there's some esoteric mystery to barbecue—a secret sauce, the wood, or aging or marinating the meat—hell, no! You just gotta know what you want."

Dennis grinned again, and took another puff of his cigarette. "Look, y'all just dig up the appropriate animal—Hawg, water buffalo, footbawhl, Jimmy Hoffa, whatever—and you cook it until you can pull the bones out." He paused for dramatic effect.

"Then?" I prompted.

"Then—" (George gave Dennis a quick, conspiratory smirk)— "you cook it some moahhh'!"

"Uh-huh, sure do," his buddy enthused, "till it falls awwhhf th'bone."

"Or awhhff your plate. Then, y'all scare up some coleslaw . . . possibly some cawhhnbread—"

"Gotta have that cawhhnbread—"

"Well, yeah, Ah'd say so, but you really gotta have that coleslaw—"

"Oh, well, yeah—"

"A few sixpacks . . . kegs, even . . . ahn' some serious booze."

"Bourbon, maybe—the real stuff. The kinda animal these piss-ants ain't nevvuh met in their lahhhvs."

"Oh yeah—Maker's Mash . . . Rebel Yell . . . Ol' Welluh—"

"Ah suppose we could let 'em get away with Wahld Turkey—"

"Could do, seein' as how they cay-yant lay ahold of the real stuff, an' wouldn't know what to look foah' even if they could—"

"Nuh-UHHH! Waste good mash awhn a Yankee? Shee-yit fahhr, bawh!"

"Ahn' finally, y'all invahht EVRUHBODY!"

"Oh yeah!"

"Good Ol' Bawhs, Rednecks, lotsa girls, Dawgs, pool-hawhl hustluhs, stockcar racers, moonshahnuhs, an' anybody y'all happen to be related to—"

"Thass goddamn near the whole county, bawh—"

"Shee-yit, yeah, ahn' evruhbody else around, lahhk maybe a few of you sorry-ass Yankees—provahdin', a'course, y'all bring some likkuh and a sense'a hyew-muh!"

"Oh, YEAAHHH!"

"Ahn' that," cackled George victoriously, "is Real Barbecue!"

Dennis hung his head and smiled sort of sheepishly. "Figures, if you cay-yan't fahhnd a little ol' run-down joint with th'boards fawhllin' awhffa it an' an authentic sahhn out front sayin' 'BAR-B-Q,' by the sahhd of a ol' dirt road, then you best roast yowh own animal yowh *own*-self."

George scratched his ear thoughtfully. "Better that way anyhow," he opined.

I thought about that for a long time. "Gentlemen," I told them, "it occurs to me that we haven't been talking about food at all."

They rolled sleepy, sated eyes at me through a cloud of smoke, and waited. "Y'all been talking about *home*."

Dennis and George sighed, smiling, in gentle unison.

"Yeahhhh," they breathed, "reckon we have."

Didn't have nothing to do with Hawg at all.

Of course, I do recall a time when the animal in question had everything to do with it. It was back in the spring of '82, and one of the residence halls on the campus of my school on Long Island had been put on probation—again—for an indiscretion involving burst water mains, surfboards, some cafeteria trays, and the flooding of the entire ground floor of the hall. The denizens thereof, it must be understood, were a quasi-legal fraternity of Footbawhl-playing, beer-guzzling, female-molesting partiers generally known as the Cellar Dwellers, or the Riggs Hall Piggs. That day of infamy, therefore, became known as The Day The Riggies Piggies Went Surfing.

The Head Pigg was a six-foot-seven-inch behemoth who answered to David "DB" Radley. He was big, blond, and from Alabama, with a grin as great as original sin, and knuckles the size of walnut shells. His best buddy—and Vice Pigg—was Tommy

Lee "T-Bone" Austen. He was big. He was blond. He, however, was from Georgia. Like most Deep South boys, though, they were both amiable, laconic, and slow-tempered—until irritated.

DB and T-Bone were irritated. "Probation" meant no more drag races in the Quad. No more Toga an' Moonshahn soirées. No more magical, intoxicating nights hunting for the Last Virgin On Long Island. The Piggies were devastated. Their morale was zip. Something had to be done—and quickly—before the semester ended in disgrace and ignominy. Something original, exciting, and guaranteed to either make them Legends or get them expelled. Or both, preferably.

"Bawhs," drawled DB, "we need a barbecue."

Barbecues are usually fairly innocuous affairs, but not when they involve revenge, a Southerner, and a few hundred of his closest friends. Everything was fine, though—until the steers arrived.

DB grinned. DB and his blood brothers dug a pit the size of the Suez Canal in the middle of the lawn outside of Riggs Hall, and filled it with charcoal, newspaper, and hickory branches. DB then built two gigantic Y-frame rotisseries, and stuck a steer on each. And finally, DB sent out his invitations—and waited.

And they arrived, in droves, on that Friday afternoon: every jock, redneck, biker, and misfit within a two-hundred-mile radius . . . lugging girlfriends, tents, kegs, footbawhls, booze, frisbees, backpacks—anything that could conceivably enliven the proceedings. They came, from near and far—to watch the steers roast.

Steers take a long time and a lot of booze to cook. By nightfall, the second shift of steer-turners and steer-basters were in position, while the air was splintered with the screams, gasps, giggles, and groans of Footbawhl and fornication in high gear. And DB just sat there, with his barbecue permit in one hand and a beer in the other, smiling sweetly and unhelpfully at the campus administrator who couldn't quite fathom how a few friends, a grill, and a couple of pounds of meat could ever evolve into this.

"Ah didn't say whut *kahhhhnd* of meat," explained DB.

By noon the next day, the steers were almost done, and so were the revelers. Five shifts of turners and basters had by now collapsed under the weight of their awesome responsibility. Even so, willing hands continued to take up the slack. By four o'clock the village was emptied of beer, and kegs had to be sent for from the next town; and by five o'clock T-Bone and his crew began rolling empty oil drums up the hill to Riggs Hall.

"What," gasped the embattled administrator, "are *those* for?"

There's still a hole in the Riggs Hall lawn, and although DB and the bawhs are all gone now, there are still some Piggies who swear by their kegs that on the last weekend of the spring semester, you can hear the strains of Charlie Daniels swelling on the humid wind, smell the slow sizzle of roasting steer, and hear DB tell the administrator, with a perfectly straight face:

"Fo' th'bahhbecue sawwhhse—whut else!"

Ain't got *nuthin'* to do with Hawg at *all*.

15 *Quiche Mah Eye!*

Conversion, as I said, is an ugly, insidious business—and strictly one-way. I thought that once a Yankee got herself back over the Maryland-Delaware border, she'd safely revert back to her indigenous proclivities, native tongue, and Seventh Avenue clothes. Not so. Undefiled Urban Yankeedom becomes a thing of the past—as long as there's a Dixie Man, Nouvelle Cuisine, and some socially myopic Yankees to complicate her life.

We had made the tactical error of eating out. It being New York, in the heart of the Yupper West Side, the neighborhood eateries were rife with crêpes, quiche, anything al pesto, and a slew of other fantasy foods. He studied the menu, silently, for several minutes, then snapped it down with a hiss.

"Yeahh," he snarled, "but where's the *food*?"

I made a big show of studying the wine list. Our drinking buddy Gordon, Boston-born and L.A.-bred, scanned his face with startled eyes.

"There's nothing *but* food here," he protested. "Veal Cordon Bleu, a delicate little breast of chicken in artichoke and white wine sauce, Crêpes St. Jacques—"

That's what Ah mean," he told Gordon, "there ain't nuthin' to eat."

I could feel Gordon flinch without even looking at him. At any moment, his beloved Shrimp And Crabmeat Ambrosia In Avocado Halves would come under fire, and it would be too much for him. Still, I gave him credit for having guts. He bit the inside of his cheek, gently set his drink down, and smiled, ever-so-sweetly, across the table.

"That's really an informed opinion," he purred, "from a man brought up on saltpork and cornpone."

His adversary eyed him coldly. "Yeah," he purred back, "an' Ah gotta listen to a lecture on 'real' food from a May-yan in a *pink shirt.*"

Gordon glanced at his shirt, flushed, and quickly stuck his feet under the table. His socks matched. I buried myself behind the centerpiece.

"Yes . . . well . . . we'll see about style when it comes time to order, won't we?" He bent a sardonic eyebrow in my mate's direction. "Of course, you'll probably be going hungry, seeing as how you won't eat what you can't pronounce."

A pair of brown Southern eyes scrunched into ugly slashes and microwaved Gordon to dust as he rasped, all venom, "At least Ah can ah-denti-fah what Ah or-duh."

It was at this point that Gordon wisely decided to make a phone call, and I had to excuse myself; so when we left our respective orders with our country-cured bon vivant, we had no idea what—if anything—he had decided upon.

Until the pigs' feet arrived.

"Uh-HUHHHH!" he enthused. "Ah'll say this much foah' New Yawwhhk food in the '80s—if it involves mesquite, y'all kin git it!" He sliced a knuckle expertly. "Ain't Real, but ain't half-bad, either."

"Aren't pigs' feet supposed to be pickled or something?" I asked him.

"Yeah," he allowed, "but you cay-yant count on a sorry-ass Yankee to do 'em up rahht. So Ah jus' asked 'em foah' any part of animal they hadn't already converted inta Stuffed Pawwhk Chawp Magnifique, a sports jacket, or toxic waste, an' to do what they could t'save it."

It was Gordon's moment to roll smug blue eyes and gloat mightily. "Typical!" he brayed. "All Southern food—made from *parts* of animals! Chitlins, pigs' feet, ham hocks—all *parts*!"

It was also a very brief moment, as a pretty red-headed waitress appeared, all freckles and smiles. "Ah spoke t'th'chef, an' b'tween th'two-a us, we rustled up some of these." She set down a steaming platter of hickory-smoked ribs. "Made do with what we gawwht. But Ah hope y'all come back real soon, now . . . "

He watched her retreating derrière appreciatively, beaming all the while. "Texas," he explained. "Close enough."

I watched Gordon's face fall about twenty feet as the other man dug happily into the smoking pile. He smiled at us compassionately, then flipped Gordon a thick, juicy rib.

"Well, as that Yankee fast food commercial of yours says," he smirked, "'Parts is parts'!"

Somehow, Gordon's quiche was never the same for him.

Ever again.

vii. Kinfolks

16 *Generations*

James Baldwin once wrote a piece for the *New York Times* on Black English, in which he said that language "is the most vivid and crucial key to identity: it reveals the larger private identity and connects one with, or divorces one from, the larger, public or commercial identity."

The most vivid, perhaps, but not necessarily the most revealing. Southern speech—and all its variations—is unique in that there's still enough actively used idiom in it to link twentieth century vernacular directly with its seventeenth-century roots, with the very history of its speakers. Far more illuminating than the spoken word, however, is the way in which Southerners remember their history—not so much how they say things, but how they recall them.

History is usually written by the winning side, but it is always best remembered by the losers. We were talking about the history of the James River when suddenly his eyes lit up to about a billion watts.

"And did you hear?" he burst out, "They burnt th'T'baccah Exchange down! To the ground! To the very *ground!*"

I rolled that piece of information around in my head for a moment. I had just been to Shockoe Slip in Richmond the previous day, and didn't recall seeing any tobacco exchanges—charred or intact. Still . . .

"Really?" I replied, "and who did that?"

His smile iced over as a sudden Arctic avalanche crashed down on me.

"*Benedict Awwhhnuld*," he hissed, "who else?" I winced into my hands as he bounced from foot to foot, gesticulating wildly.

"Oh, yeahh!" he enthused, "He marched down the rivvuh an' up an' FAHRRED th'banks! Yes! He done RAY-YUZZED Richmond, Vah-ginn-yuh, to th' ground!"

He took a long pull of his beer, wiped his lips, and, struggling for breath, took up his tale again. "Ohhhh, Lawwwhhd, th'flames jus' shot inta th'sky, an' th'tra-duhs fled in terruh, an' the horses stampeded, an' there wa'n't nowheah to run! An' one thing aftuh anuthuh jus' up an' caught fahr lahhk kindlin'! Gawwd Awh-mahhty, it was hellacious!"

I bit my lip and suppressed a smirk, but my acerbic little Yankeeness got the better of me. "Oh? Were you there, personally?" I purred.

His glower sliced right through me. "*Ah* didn't *have* to be."

And come to think of it, he didn't. History for Southerners is as real and alive for them as the day it was made, particularly so if a relative was there to witness the event. I would be tempted to add that all history is that way for them, but it isn't—only Southern or family history. Which *is* all history, I guess. Still, he had been taught the trials and tribulations of Dixie thoroughly—if somewhat colorfully—so I couldn't really dispute the accuracy of his version. I could, however, look somewhat askance at it.

"Yeah, that ol' Benedict Awwhnuld," he chuckled, "he was a terruh, he was. Bad enough that he was a shiftless, no-'count sumbitch t'begin with, but to up ahn' sell out t'th'British—Jaysus!" He rolled his eyes, overcome with his own narrative. "An' then t' burn down Richmun'!" His breath came out in a long, fluttering sigh as he shook his head and lamented:

"Ah jus' knew that bawh would go to th'bahhhd!"

It's that personal "*Ah*-know-Ah-was-*there*" quality that so amuses me about Southerners, that utter conviction they have about their history as they do about their religion, and the ferocity with which they defend both. But for all that blood-proud intensity, they nonetheless have a certain fuzziness about dates—as if the relevance of an event reduces the need to cubbyhole it with an actual date. I guess there really isn't that great a need for chronology when you think about it, since all Southerners operate on a first-name basis with God and most major historical figures, anyway. But in any case, writer Christopher Hallowell once observed that trappers in the bayous of Louisiana measured time in storms—that a certain camp was built "just before

Betsy hit" (the summer of 1965), or that a panther was killed in the palmettos when the hurricane of 1915 descended upon them. Roy Reed recalled in "Ab Snopes Makes Good" that the act of replacing an old barn plank pulled him back to the day his neighbor nailed it to what was then his barn—and the same neighbor, upon digging up an onion from his garden, recalled how his grandmother brought the original seed in a towsack from Tennessee to Hogeye, Arkansas, over a hundred years before. Neither man, however, could supply actual dates.

But so what? History should be remembered for what it was, not when, and for what it actually means—unless, of course, you have on your hands five or six Tab-crazed Yuppies battling to the death over a round of Trivial Pursuit; then, perhaps, numbers are important. But by and large, remembering who did what and why, who is related to whom and, from there, who they themselves all are, is really what constitutes history to a son (or daughter) of the South.

This leads, naturally, to the subject of clans. Southerners revel in their heritage and they revel in their families, so any chance to elevate a kinsman into the ranks of Legend is a doubly gratifying experience. However, should an ancestor fail to attain epic heights in his lifetime by virtue of, say, fate, circumstance, or just plain incorrigibility, then the next best thing is to make him larger than life when he departs this earth. No Southern kinsman is ever so cherished as when he is dead—properly dead—so that everybody can then wail and moan and inflate his memory to Mythic Proportions.

I saw the wailing and moaning operatives in full swing one crisp spring day, when a friend and I went with Her Mama, Her Aunt, Her Cousin, and the blessings of their male kinfolk to tend the grave of Her Mama's Mama. It was an icy-eyed, clenched-lipped entourage which set out, picnic basket in hand, but it was an entirely different group of women who surfaced once we reached the gravesite. Her Mama was the first to succumb.

"Mama! Mama!" she howled, "Awwwhhhh, Lawwwhd, whah didju have t'take her?"

The hairs on my neck stood up as the flesh beneath them puckered up, crawled and twitched. I rolled an uncertain eye at Jayne.

"What the hell's going on?" I muttered.

"Watch," she mumbled back. "It gets better."

It did. Her Aunt then stepped forward and, throwing herself down on the grass, clutched the headstone and shrieked to the heavens, "Awwhhh, Gawwd, whah'dju have t'go? Whah'dju ev-vuh leave us, Mama? Ohhhhh, Mama—mah poah' sweet Mama!"

Jayne's mother shook her head sadly. "She was, wa'n't she? Sweetest woman who evvuh drew breath."

"Oh, you know it, Faye. A good, Christian, God-fearin' wo-man—"

"A real lady, honey—"

"Oh, chile, was she evvuh—despite her havin' to raise us-all—"

"Didn't have no dahh-muns or fancy clothes, but you jus' knew she was Quality all th'same—"

"Ohhhh, poah' ol' Mama—"

"Poah' ol' Mama—"

And then they both wept. At length. And copiously, doubt-lessly calling upon God to admire their filial grief, while we three younger women devoted conspicuous minutes to the study of our shoes, the grass, or anything else even vaguely removed from the scene before us. Suddenly, Jayne began to smirk, as Her Mama looked up, smiling brightly.

"Well," Faye chirped, "now that we gawwht that done with, we'd best be gettin' awhhn with th'house-keepin'."

She bustled over to her big woven workbasket, and handed Pauli her complement of brushes, rags, and the fresh flowers to be arranged. Her sister nodded shortly and went to work.

"You see?" whispered Jayne, "the day wasn't a total waste."

I crucified her on a single look. "For whom?" I hissed back.

Jayne blinked sparkling, innocent eyes at me. "Whah chile," she drawled evenly, "foah' *them*, of course!"

She had a point. Both women were obviously enjoying their keening immensely, as it involved reminiscing about their mother, gossiping about their relatives, and occasionally pinning matching sets of flinty blue eyes on Jayne and Eunice and admon-ishing, "Now jus' you remembuh whut a saint yowh' Nanna was, su-guh!"

"Nanna," Eunice softly growled to her cousin, "was a barra-cuda in Support-Hose."

"Uh-huh," breathed Jayne, "a barracuda with a mean back-hand." Their mothers plowed on, unheeding.

"She was the soul'a kahhndness," asserted Faye, as she dusted the headstone.

"Y'all could allus turn t'Mama when you were in trouble," replied Pauli.

"Whah!" her sister exclaimed, "she was even kahhnd t'th Robertson folks!"

Pauli glanced up from her sweeping, startled. "What, them folks whose kids trahhd t'burn down our barn one year?"

"The self-same ones."

Pauli considered that point quickly. "So she was," she conceded. She leveled a baleful glare at her niece. "Even to them West Coast hippie-trash and othuh low-lahhff frien's'a yours."

Jayne smiled tightly. "Here comes the history lesson," she mumbled. Eunice coughed politely and looked away.

"Mama was th'bravest woman Ah evvuh knew," said Pauli. "'Course, you two doan remembuh this—" (the two cousins shifted uncomfortably) "—but Mama done held awhhf the revenuahs from yowh' Grand-daidy's still durin' th'Depression—"

"Was our only source'a income went th'fahhhm went broke, hard tahhms back," said Faye.

"Nursed half th'blessed county when we all come down wi'black tongue an' awhll th'cattle started dah-yin' awhhff—"

"Doan fuh-git th'diptree—"

"Ohhh, Lawwhd, th'diptree!—"

"'Diptree'?" I asked.

"She means diphtheria," Jayne clarified, "black tongue was cholera."

"Wa'n't nuthin' could kill Mama."

"Nuthin' but Gawd Hi'self."

"Gawwd, she was a pow-wuhful healin' woman—"

"Pow-wuhful, honey! An' a dead shot, an' a mean hand at splittin' lawgs, killin' hawgs, an' mos' anythin' else—"

"An'," thundered Pauli, as the two girls jumped, "she, pil-luh of th' Valosta New Lahhht Baptis' Chu'ch, was the mos' rahhtchus, Bahble-readin', Gawd-fearin' woman you could evvuh hope t'know in this or any othuh lahhff-time!"

Her sister pondered that one for a few seconds. "Yeahhhh," she allowed, "but she was a fiend when th'local trash gawwht ugly. I remembuh Mama done run, oh, 'bout ten, twelve, mebbe two-dozen of them common low-lahhfs offa her land wi' jus' her broomstick."

"Which she didn't happen to be riding at the time," observed Jayne.

Her mother stuck her hands on her hips.

"Now, Mama," said her daughter, soothingly, "was that before she personally put down Nat Turner's rebellion, or aftuh she done ran the Yankee carpetbagguhs outta th'South?"

"You hush yowh' mouth now, girl," warned Her Mama. Faye sighed and rolled sorrowful eyes at me. "Ah jus' wish you'd known Mama, but she up an' dahhhd so suddenly. Mah poah' fam'ly is still grievin'."

I nodded and looked appropriately disappointed. "I bet," I told her. "But when exactly did she pass away?"

She clutched her heart and wiped away a frail tear. "Oh, Jay-sus!" she moaned, "it was jus' a short piece ago!"

"Oh?" I stammered, "earlier this year?"

Pauli bent her head and covered her face with her hands. "Eighteen years ago," she rasped, brokenly, "jus' lahhk yes-tuhdday!"

And began to wail, with her sister, yet again.

Jayne took a deep breath and crept back towards the car, Eunice in tow.

"An' y'know," she said, "there're actually some Yankees still wonderin' if we're *still* fahhhtin' th'War."

"Fighting the War?" I shot back, "You folks are still rowing the Ark!" Eunice grinned, all braces and spittle. "Yeahhh, we were there foah' that, too. An' we'll allus be fahhtin' th'War, Ah reckon," she vowed, "lawwwhng as there's a Suth-nuh alahhv to tell you how it *really* happened!"

It didn't end there. Driving back home, the two mothers began working on whom to invite for their Mama's upcoming Memorial.

"Y'all remembuhed Jim Hawthorne ahn' his three, didn't you?" asked Faye. Her sister pulled a face.

"'Course Ah did, though Gawd only knows whah you want them . . . *po-its* around."

"They're kin!"

"They trash!"

"That may be," reasoned Faye, "but they're our trash."

Pauli grunted contemptuously. "Jus' barely."

Faye chilled her with a frosty eye. "Who was Mama's half-sis-tuh?" she asked.

Her sibling glowered. "Aint Bea, a'course."

"Rahht. An' who was Aint Bea's least chile?"

"Cousin Sybil," muttered Pauli, tightly. Faye smiled sweetly at her, unfazed.

"An' Cousin Sybil's husbin'?" she prodded.

Her sister let out an aggravated sigh. "Jim evvuh-lovin' Hawthorne." She caught the younger woman's triumphant smirk, and finished the thought. "An' Sybil's children are half-Austen, too, an' are our half second-cousins, even if their Dai-dy is slahhhm an' up an' left poah' ol' Sybil, which means we gawwhtta have Sybil an' her new husbin', too, an' their seven—foah' of which, Ah'm sure you recawwhhl, jus' happen t'be his outta that Sarah James, who you *know* full well is that Lasiva James' hussy of a dawwhh-tuh who done slept with gawddahm near ev'ry May-yan in th'county!"

Faye thought about that. "Lasiva done run awhhff with that half-wahhld Indian-faced May-yan from th'hills, didn't she?"

"Naww, that was Shir-*lee* Cobbs. Lasiva done took up with that May-yan, but was Shir-*lee* what got him in th'end." Pauli beamed pure venom on her sister. "Now you still sure y'all want all this kin at th'Memorial?"

"Yep," said Faye. "'Cause near as we can tell, the father of that self-same Sarah was Aint Bea's Dai-dy—" she pinned her sister to the ground with a laser-beam glare, "which makes Sybil's second husbin's children our thuhhd cousins ANYWAY!"

It was a long time before anyone dared to speak. Finally, Pauli glanced up and searched her younger sister's face.

"You sure?" she whispered.

Faye nodded slowly. Pauli just sighed. "Awhhrahht. Foah' Hawthornes, nahhn Moores or Austens or whatevvuh th'hell they are, the real remainin' Austens, three Pickens ahn' foah' Lees."

"Uh-huh," Faye concurred, "plus Uncle Bob Ray an' Lois an' their foah', Grandai-dy Nelson's fawstuh-bruthuh Auggie, an' awhhl th'othuh Nelson half-cousins we kin round up." She grinned mischievously. "Does that make 'em half-Nelsons, you reckon?"

Pauli cackled. "Half-Nelsons! Hehhehhehhehheh!"

"Fam'ly history bin one lawwhng wrestle an' tussle, anyways."

"Sho' nuff has."

"So?" asked Faye.

"So," surrendered Pauli, "they family." She turned around in her seat and shook her head wryly. "You mus' think we're crazy, trahh-yin' t'figure out who b'lawwhhngs t'who, an' who exac'ly is kin."

No," I answered, "but it must drive you crazy."

"That ain't so," her sister interjected. "We remembuh it fahhn. It's important."

"You Yankee folk remembbuh your roots an' your hist'ry through books," added Pauli. She paused, and looked from her sister to her daughter to her niece. "We-all remembuh through our people."

Living history.

17 Jus' Plain Folks

William Faulkner, while a visiting professor at the University of Virginia, once remarked that he loved Virginians because they were all snobs: "... and I like snobs. A snob (spends) so much time being a snob, that he has little time to meddle with you."

A somewhat harsh observation. Nevertheless, somewhere, way above the strata of Good Ol' Bawhs, Rednecks, Southern Preppies and Suth'un Gennelmun in general, exists the crustiest layer of the American upper crust. Oh, sure, Palm Beach has its matrons—as do San Fran, Dallas, New York, and Philly—but Virginia has the only social elite that dares claim direct descent from God. Louisiana and the Carolinas have their own First Families, heaven knows; but any First Family of Virginia member worth his plantation naturally reserves a certain disdain for such climbers, half of whom are probably descendants of some jumped-up planter's bastard, *anyway*. Or so he believes. What an FFV thinks of the Brahmins of Boston is anybody's guess.

In any case, the FFVs are here to stay. The bulk of the white South is descended from the Ulster Scots—the Scotch-Irish Protestants of Northern Ireland who fled that country, as they did Scotland before that, to escape religious, economic, and political persecution at the hands of the English. The Scots—and some English—who poured into Belfast did so, with the blessings of the Crown, to "colonize" Catholic Ireland; but even though the Scotch-Irish were as Protestant as their sovereign, they were the wrong kind of Protestant—they were Presbyteri-

ans, while the Court of St. James was Church of England. *Anglicans.* Hence the steady trans-Atlantic stream of unwanted Celts to the U.S. The Catholic Irish came in droves, too, no question; but the Protestant Irish—or Scotch-Irish, to be precise—came first. And they came to the wide-open South.

Of course, the English had come before them. As early as 1607, actually. And once the Crown realized what a treasure trove it had in this new land called Virginia (which, at the time encompassed about six present-day states), they quickly dispatched royal governors to rule it, and a newly-created aristocracy to cultivate it. Hence the FFVs, whose ancestors thoughtfully brought along with them their fellow Englishmen as indentured servants—before the Crown got the really bright idea of shipping off its surplus criminals to help populate and work the land.

But old habits die hard, so despite Thomas Jefferson, the Bill of Rights, and the abolition of slavery, the FFVs continue to flourish—as governors, senators, planters, captains of industry, and philanthropists—and, for the most part, to their credit and the benefit of their Commonwealth. So perhaps they should be pardoned their snobbery.

Should be. Except for the fact that, like any other pictures of pomposity, they provide far too much material for their more common brethren to resist working with. Will Rogers, for one, cracked that the Prince of Wales was born in Richmond. Richmond, England—he didn't have enough ancestors to be born in Richmond, Virginia. And H.L. Mencken dipped his pen in acid to note: "... the old aristocracy went down the red gullet of war. ... Urbanity, *politesse*, chivalry? It was in Virginia that they invented the device of searching for contraband whiskey in ladies' underwear!"

In all fairness, though, to the FFVs—or FFNCs, FFLs or FFGs—they still produce what many women consider to be the most eligible bachelors in the Continental U.S. Being able to identify and ensnare one of these aforementioned gentlemen should therefore be crucial to any aspiring Debutantes, Belles, Matrons, or First Ladies out there:

Identifying Suth'un Gennelmun

(1) They all drawl. (Even the Philadelphian ones.)
(2) They don't know what greenbacks look like.
(3) They do, however, know how they work.
(4) Only because one of their ancestors is on one.
(5) They all have ancestral homes, with ancestral acreage.
(6) The size of an emerging nation.
(7) And they always have horses. Lots of 'em.

There are numerous little tip-offs in their conversation, too. For instance, beginning their sentences with: "Well, when great-great-great-grand-Dai-dy Edmonds was alahhhv an' still owned Naw' Carolahnnuh. ... "; announcing they'll be heading for their Albemarle County spreads for the week "since Wawshin'tun gets so dreary after a dozen or so receptions"; or inviting you to Kentucky next weekend to see his colt run. In the Derby. Spotting more than ten monuments, street signs, or public buildings with his family name on them is likewise a dead giveaway.

Ensnaring Suth'un Gennelmun. For Keeps.

(1) Make sure you own jodhpurs, and a pair of long, white gloves.
(2) Know, first, what jodhpurs are.
(3) And never wear the two together.
(4) Know your Guide To Perfect Belledom, and use it.
(5) Say, innocently, "You mean great-great-Aint Mary Sue-Ellen's fawstuh-muthuh's brother, *Charles Puh-cee* Edmonds? *That* Edmonds?"
(6) Ask him if he, too, will be attending so-and-so's Bash Of The Season and then:
(7) Give him permission to take you. (Before he asks to.)
(8) Complain about the servants.

This will, naturally, indicate to him that you are a Lady who knows How Things Are Done, and is therefore entitled to expect the finer things in life. From him. On a permanent basis. He knows perfectly well that Belles have been programmed as much as he has been programmed—to be gallant, chivalrous, protective of all females, and generally to look after them, support them, and do for them, while they look gorgeous and file their nails. He understands this. Belles understand that they must be outwardly sweet, supportive, unassuming, and prone to producing heirs, while not letting on that they might actually have an original thought in their heads (which, they know, would alarm and bewilder the menfolk). They are to run the house and run the men, whether they know it or not, and to never let them doubt for an instant that they are Lord and Master. Even if yours is a drunken, half-civilized lout of a chauvinist. Just as long as *you* now understand this.

Where They Can Be Found

(1) Out fox-hunting.
(2) Out ruling.
(3) Out mixing (with othhuh Gennelmun).
(4) At the White House (or General Assembly, at least).
(5) Wherever Southern Belles are, dressed for the kill.

You might also case Newport News and the Hampton area, on the off-chance they're visiting their yachts. Another approach, however, instead of competing head-on with Real Belles, would be to Find, Isolate, and Charm His Mama To Death. Or, if you're really enterprising, Their Dai-dies. But be careful. That route is not without its own pitfalls.

But Suth'un Gennelmun, after all, need love, too (or a reasonable facsimile thereof); and being dutiful sons and patriots, have a pressing need to perpetuate the family name. So consider your involvement in that venture a public service. Remember, it's not an entirely thankless task—and somebody just has to do it. The legend of *le beau sabreur* must ride on.

18 *The Crinoline Conspiracy*

One cannot discuss Southern Men without mentioning Southern Women; one is, after all, essential in the production of the other. However, in all fairness to these good women, I think it only right to point out that you can't blame them for their menfolk—bear in mind, rather, that their men probably made them the way they are.

The Way They Are comes in two forms: Southern Women, and that mind-boggling cultural aberration known as the Southern Belle.

Southern Women are Real Women: they cook, clean, shop, raise kids, hold down jobs, run the house, sometimes work the farm, and—most importantly—survive the Southern Male . . . all at the same time. In another life, they did all of this without the benefit of modern conveniences, electricity, or day care, as well as managing to fight off a marauding Indian, redcoat or damyankee soldier or two, to boot. In this life, too, some of their great-great granddaughters have known the same kind of back-breaking labor, the same kind of grinding, gruelling way of life that can bleed a person white; all of these women—past and present—command my respect.

I did say some of their daughters—not all. Interwoven with these embodiments of virtuous Southern womanhood, there came to exist a race of females so outrageously egocentric and superficial, so flamboyantly hedonistic and venal, that all other women paled in comparison. These are, of course, the ladies of leisure, the plantation princesses—the Southern Belles.

I confess I have a grudging admiration for them. All Southern women possess a truly horrific set of survival skills, but the Belles have perfected their talents and elevated them to a fine art. They had to—they have Southern Men.

Their hustler's instinct, their indisputable genius for extracting the most of anything, at any time, from any male, is probably what kept these ladies alive through centuries of revolution, civil war, and their own menfolk. Their sisters in other cities are not without their own ability—the Brahmin Belles of Boston, New York JAPs and sundry WASPrincesses from coast to coast—but not one of them can match the Southern Belle's peerless gift for achieving with a flickering eyelash or Clara Bow pout whatever her little heart desires . . . achieving with that scant weaponry what it takes the others nagging, sulking, guilt-tripping, or tantrum-throwing to pull off. In this, the Belle is matchless.

Blanche DuBois was a failed one. Liz Taylor was a manufactured one. And Scarlett O'Hara was the ultimate, quintessential Belle, the ninja-keen instincts wrapped in a frappé of hooped skirts and sweet killer smile. But even without the benefit of ruffles, the Southern Belle is still recognizable—and still a force to be reckoned with.

What It Takes

(1) Plastic
(2) Dai-dy's
(3) Your own rope of pearls
(4) Lip-pouting ability
(5) Long eyelashes
(6) Plenty of all of the above

Looking helpless never hurts, either. Let me emphasize the "looking" part—Belles are never helpless. Never have been, and never will be. In fact, Belles are probably the most self-reliant, capable women on earth, lace-fan mentality notwithstanding. Sure, they can haul their own laundry and lug fifty pounds of groceries home just like anyone else, but who among them would be caught dead doing so, when a quivering eyelash or gossamer sigh will instantly galvanize a herd of stunned males into performing these and any other of a number of functions?

It works like this. Southern Belle wants something done. Even

if she's that strange anomaly known as Working (gasp!) Southern Belle, she'll still be able to pull off this stunt—Belledom transcends income brackets. The pearls will peep discreetly from under her shirt collar and she'll bite her lip delicately as—with equal delicacy—she flexes her fingers into her maybe-not-white-but-real-kid-nonetheless gloves, and, with just an evvuh-so subtle look of helpless bewilderment, she bats her lashes and looks around for the nearest white knight to dispatch her errand with speed, efficiency, and gallantry. Blink, blink.

And he will. Because the Belle knows better than any intellectual, psychologist, feminist, or the wisest mother alive that there is absolutely nothing in the world a man cannot be made to do with a light touch of feminine connivance. The hell with the equality stuff—men were put on this earth to do for them, and if all it takes to get them to deliver is to turn your incandescent eyes on full and smile, well, then, why not? Belles, in their way, are bigger feminists than the most prolific bra-burner ever was. They think nothing of turning the tables and keeping a man in his theoretical place, stepping and fetching, keeping the Belles amused, and generally doing all the rotten, second-class citizen things that *men* have had women do for centuries—it's only fair. And the only "sell-out" involved is that of looking beautiful and acting incapable.

That's probably what incenses non-Belles the most. The looking beautiful bit is bad enough, but it's the Simper Factor which really gets them. What gets to them even more, though, is how well it works. There is, without doubt, a very fine line between Belle and Bimbo, and for a generation of women brought up to gag on the Madonna/Whore Syndrome, it's sometimes too much to stomach. Let us not, however, forget the element of envy— there's something unquestionably wicked and wonderful and thoroughly enjoyable about being able to crook one's finger, and step over the prostrate forms of grown men groveling on the gravel, foaming and writhing at one's feet . . . that kind of power . . . not unlike a lot of male fantasies. . . .

So, okay, you're willing to sell your feminist soul for a little of that power. So there are a few things you should know first:

(1) Eyes Are Everything.

Belle Eyes flirt. They bat—in feigned confusion, helplessness, and genteel mortification. Occasionally, they pop up a little in polite horror, and very occasionally they tear up a tad and pout, but that's purely an emergency measure. Belle Eyes nevvuh squint. They never get puffy, have rings or grow crows' feet, and they nevvuh—Scarlett aside, because she was a wild one—skewer a victim with fiery fury. They *can*, however, scathe the aforementioned target with a look of icy contempt: a certain effortless, frosty disdain which is perfectly appropriate, should a so-called gentleman do something really awwwhhful and . . . well . . . you *know* . . . *tacky*. Like forget his plastic.

(2) Pout Or Be Dahhhmmed.

So he won't take you to the Farmington Hunt, because of his heart transplant yesterday. So this year's entire social season is out, since he was tacky enough to get kidnapped by Democratic

terrorists. So he *won't* buy you your sixth fur of the year. So . . .
you pout. Carefully. Drop those eyes a touch, stick out those lips,
and sigh a lot. Wistful. Grieving. How could he *evvuh* refuse you?
(Si-iii-iiigggghhhh. . . .) Dai-dy jus' doan love his Su-guh no
moah'. . . .

(3) Drawling (optional).

You can, if you're a non-Southern Belle, try the High-Pitched
And Breathless Approach, the Sultry, Throaty Rasp, or the Coy
Ingenue Tactic. Nothing, but nothing, though, can ever come
close to the syrupy, molasses-slow Drawwwwhhl that is the
Southern Belle's by birthright. He'll stand there and take it.
Every word of it. There's something disarming and mesmerizing
about a sawwhhfft, oval-edged vawhse jus' wrappin' i'self
around a May-yan lahhhk layers of silken, sun-warmed, magno-
lia-scented quilts. . . . Lawwhhhdy, Lawwhhdy. . . . Even if she *is*
oozing venom.

It's the Rabbit/Headlight Cause and Effect Syndrome. Rabbits don't have too much to do all day except eat, sleep, and make
more rabbits, so every now and then, just for the hell of it, they
dash from the boring safety of the woods and leap out in front of
the nearest car. They get flattened, sure, but those few splintered nanoseconds when they are paralyzed in delicious terror,
with an orgasmic adrenalin overload frying their little rodent
brains, probably make their entire existences worthwhile. Not
unlike men in Major Lust. Southern Belles know this; it is therefore just a question of deciding on the correct ploy: the intense
Headlight Effect, or the subtler, more hypnotic Velvet Snake
Gambit. Lah-dee-dahhhhh. . . .

(4) Nevvuh Carry Cash.

(5) Nevvuh Carry ANYTHING. . . .

(6) . . . Heavier Than A Rope of Pearls.

These denote you as a Lady—Demure, Genteel, and otherwise
Well-Bred. You'll need your pearls: to toy with, at your throat,
to toss over your shoulder as you flounce off in a fit of pique, to
drape tastefully at your décolletage, or to nibble on, pearl by
pearl, as you look helpless and distracted and . . . pearls are a
must. No Belle over the age of ten would be caught dead without
hers.

(7) Make Sure You Know All The Best Stores, and

(8) Always Charge It To Dai-dy.

Dai-dy is an all-purpose male. He could be your Dai-dy for real, or he could just be your Su-guh Dai-dy. Or Big Dai-dy, Dai-dy Warbucks, Dai-dy Lawwhng-Legs—who cares? Just as long as he, that useful male between the ages of eighteen and infinity, is some kahhnd'a Gennulmin. With bucks. And is *your* Dai-dy.

Belles—Their Natural Habitats

    (1) In front of a full-length mirror.
    (2) Plantations.
    (3) Inaugural Balls.
    (4) Any expensive store.
    (5) In bed. Past noon. *Alone.*

Southern Belles go pretty much where Old Money, Taste, the Good Life, and the Right Kind Of People go. Perhaps it would be easier to delineate where they don't go:

    (1) The gym
    (2) Supermarkets
    (3) Public schools and
    (4) Subways (not even transplanted Belles).

Why they don't frequent the last three places goes without saying. But why, in an age where health, fitness, and Nautilus narcissism permeates all classes of American society, does the Belle—unlike her sister-JAPs—avoid health clubs?

It could be the climate, or something in the dawwg-wood, perhaps. The Southern climate is not generally conducive to producing decathletes among its young womanhood. The actual truth is three-fold: the Belle does not need to exercise because, first of all, it's tacky, and second, she's perfect already . . . and third, she keeps in shape through Belle Exercises. These are a fiercely-guarded set of cultural calisthenics passed down, like hemophilia, in the genes, or through barely-whispered oral tradition: a murmur here, an arched eyebrow there, and the unstated rule that a Lady should *nevvuh* attempt to do anything more strenuous than adjusting her jewelry—let alone perspire. That would be just so . . . well . . . one hates to say it . . . tacky.

Belle Exercises

    (1) Flirting   (200 calories per hour)
    (2) Pouting   (350)

(3) Being Seen	(450)
(4) Shopping	(600)
(5) Getting Dressed	(800)
(6) Admiring Oneself	(1000) (this takes longer)

Simpering, lip-pursing, smiling, lash-batting, etc., all count as Flirting. Pearl-wearing (a good aerobic exercise if you wear enough ropes) can either count as Flirting, Getting Dressed, or Being Seen. It can also be incorporated into your Admiring Oneself Regimen.

Belledom, as I said, transcends wealth; you're either born with Belle Instincts or you're not, and no amount of brass, remedial finishing school, speech lessons, or geographical transplanting will change it—to or from. It's not so terrible. Beneath that shallow, self-centered, vacuous, and narcissistic surface, lies a shallow, self-centered, and narcissistic lady just dying to be taken care of. Belles may act (or just look) vapid, but there is actually a deeply-ingrained, highly prescient peasant cunning to them all: they are methodical, manipulative, and possessed of a certain tenacious efficiency. This is what separates the true Belle from the average Bimbo—tackiness aside, Bimbos really *are* vacuous.

One of the nicest ladies I know is, by mind-set if not by upbringing, a Southern Belle. Despite her years in New York, she has always retained a tinge of antebellum mentality doubtlessly acquired from her early years in the Tidewater region of Virginia. Having a Bahhhstin-born mother didn't hurt, either. In any case, far from ameliorating any lingering streaks of ante-Belledom, life in the Big Apple brought it out in Donna in a big way: she is confident, self-reliant, and a born Extractor of Useful Things—Manhattan schist under Southern Belle lashes. She is also, for the record, by no means vacuous, frivolous, or superficial. Or stupid.

Several things tipped me off about her latent Belleness, though. For instance, she is the only woman I know outside of colonial Hong Kong who really knows How To Manage Servants; she is one of only two women I've met who doesn't look ludicrous in a hat, gloves, a rope of pearls, or other accoutrements of Belle High Dudgeon; and, most importantly, she is one of those rare women who has intimate knowledge of every major store on the eastern seaboard.

It was the week of Thanksgiving, and the radio editor on duty needed tape of stores' holiday sales across the nation. The collective brains of a half-dozen Northern Men had panned out badly, so in desperation he threw the problem onto the newsroom floor.

"Macy's," offered one writer.

"Bergdorf's," retorted an East Sider.

"Bloomie's, of course!" jumped in a third.

"Lord and Taylor's!"

"I. Magnin!"

"Gimbel's!"

"Fortunoff's!"

The editor sighed flatly. "Those are all in New York. I need some in the real world."

The Belle looked up from her computer. "What city are you lookin' foah?" she drawled pleasantly.

My radar immediately went BLIP! For a start, she never drawls unless she's about to indulge in a little Oblique Manipulation, and second, her black eyes began to crackle and snap beneath those equally black, lush lashes. I knew it was only a matter of minutes before she pounced.

The editor hesitated, sniffed, and then locked eyes with her. "Boston," he rapped out.

"Filene's," she shot back.

"Okay," he barked, "Philly."

"Wanamaker's."

"Maine."

"Talbot's, the country stawwh'a Con-cawwhhd—th'original, a'course, an'—"

"Washington!"

"Woody's—Woodward an' Lothrop!"

"Alexandria!"

"Frankie Welch's!"

"McLEAN!" he shrieked.

Donna smiled coyly. "Any stawwh in Tah-son's Cawhhnuh," she purred.

The editor blanched, gagged softly, and made a final, valiant effort.

"Atlanta, Georgia," he rasped.

Donna smiled again. Sweetly. Innocently. Smugly. She was toying with him, and he knew it. She pulled the cigarette from her lips, sipped a taste of her coffee, and pinned him with mischievous, flirtatious eyes—wide, alert, terrier-bright, ever eager to please.

"Bullock's," she breathed.

I give the guy credit. A lesser man would have wilted under her counterattack, but not Bill. He was made of sterner stuff. Not that it did him any good.

"All right," he rallied, "you're so good at stores—how about malls?"

Malls were clearly beneath a lady of her refinement, but Donna was a player. Life in New York lent a gritty, competitive edge to her more tender sensibilities. Besides, she wasn't about to be out-traveled or out-shopped. She nodded tersely.

"New York," said an anchorman.

"Roosevelt Field, Queens Plaza, King's Plaza, Greenacre an' Sun-rahhse—"

"Philly!" bleated another.

"Chestnut Hill, Brick's—but let's not fuh-get Strohbridge n' Clothiers itself—"

"Bethesda!" a writer burst out, hysterical.

"Whahht Flint."

"Quick, D.C.—mall or store!"

"Garfinkel's!" she snapped back, "an' we've hardly touched th'Beltway!"

A dozen pairs of eyes squinted at her in jagged wariness. Clearly, they were prepared to get ugly. It was Tahhm T'Play Hardbawhl.

"Richmond, Virginia," whispered a producer. The rustle of crinoline sighed on the wind, the warm magnolia smell wafted up by the lazy stir of a fan, from bygone times . . . the centuries gentled into a fuzzy blur, stopped, and slid back into themselves. . . .

"Cloverleaf Mall," she murmured.

The editor's face twitched violently as the veins pulsed in his head—spasmodic, fitful, frantic. His copy fell from his hand and he took a slow step back towards the inner studios, the Belle's eyes diamond-hard, diamond-bright . . . she wasn't done. Not by a long shot.

"Chesterfield," she teased.

"Bon Air," I replied.

"Willowlawn!" she chirped, brightening even further.

"Miller & Rhoads, Thalhimers, and the entire West End!" we screamed, in unison.

Donna threw back her head and chortled, long and loud. Obviously, she had found an unlikely kindred spirit. She dabbed her eyes even as she got wracked by the next paroxysm of gaiety, and didn't stop laughing until she spotted the editor, mutely plastered up against the studio wall. The ordeal had damn near carried him off. Donna smiled a final cherubic smile.

"Lawwwhd," she sighed, "we nevvuh even got started on the West, Southwest, Gulf Coast. . . . " Bill slumped into a shapeless hump.

"San Antone," I grinned.

"Frost's!" she chimed back. "L.A.!" A tech began dragging Bill to safety by his heels. Donna watched his prone form slide away with supranatural compassion.

"Giorgio's," I offered, "Bijan's, and all of Rodeo Drive."

"Dallas!"

"Neiman-Marcus!"

"Encino!"

"Palm Springs!"

"Chicago!" she trumpeted, her eyes on fire.

"BAL HARBOR, FLORIDA!"

"London, Hong Kong, Paris, Tokyo, Peking, Rome, Canton, Milan, Katmandu, and ISTANBUL!" we whooped, finally overcome. Donna wiped her eyes again, shook her head, and gently sighed at her computer. "GawwwdAwhh-mahhhty," she breathed, with heartfelt sincerity, "th'joys of a broad, well-rounded education!"

"Southern Belles," I replied, "don't leave home without them."

viii. Menfolks On the Move

19 If It Ain't Broke, Don't Fix It

Most women spend the better part of their relationships with their menfolk trying to get the man To Do Something. You know how that works: the lawn needs a little trim, the kitchen cabinets need new hinges . . . and you've waited all Footbawhl season for him to finally come out of hibernation, register a pulse, and re-establish a workable link between his brain and his neuromuscular system—just so he can attend to one or two of those very chores.

What the ladies fail to remember, however, is that the only thing worse than a man not doing something is, of course, A Man with a Plan. A Man Who's Got a Project. A man with vision, passion, and talent, who is guaranteed to drive any female he lives with or near absolutely crazy *by* Doing Something. Think about it. There are really only . . .

Four Natural States of Man

(1) Idle
(2) In Idle Mischief
(3) Just in Mischief
(4) Actually Doing Something

Two and Three, obviously, involve doing something. They are, however, undirected and half-hearted activities, and they are therefore not serious, dangerous, or long-lasting. They only become so when a nasty chemical interference builds up in the brain in the form of Terrific Ideas and Full-Scale Plans—and he then finds the energy and enthusiasm to carry them out. That's when he enters the final, treacherous state known as Actually Doing Something.

Southern Men are particularly susceptible to this malady. Some primeval, corpuscle-deep cry resounds in them—a red-mad, irresistible siren-call to trouble and trauma that flares up in the blood and brain and ganglia and makes Dixie Men not only want to Do Things but to Do Strange, Crazy, and Alarming Things . . . preferably involving (or at least upsetting) as many innocent bystanders as possible. Preferably female.

The floating-house project was one I've never quite recovered from. He had just spent a hectic but rewarding week smuggling grain alcohol in from Pennsylvania to energize the gallons of purple liquid chilling in the bathroom when a well-lubricated buddy sidled up to him and began urgently whispering in his ear.

I squinted at them savagely. He blinked dark, wounded deer eyes back at me. "Save the Bambi routine," I told him. "I see you, two dozen drunken Good Ol' Bawhs, and a Jacuzzi-load of strange purple alcohol eating the porcelain off of the bathtub. I also see, behind that beer stein of yours, that you are smirking." I pulled his drink away from his lips, stepped up on a footstool, and got eyeball-to-eyeball with him. "And I—just intuitively, mind you— *do not like it one bit.*"

He smoothed the smirk back into place. More or less. "Naw, naw, it's nuthin' radical," he assured me. "Dace here was just ad-mahhrin' the particular excellence of mah brew an' talking ovvuh a little business." He offered me his stein, and tucked a strand of my hair back in place. "You know sumthin'? You'll be kahhnda cute when you're fahhn-ally full-grown."

"And you'll be kind of cute," I retorted, "when you're finally sober."

I gave him a brittle smile and jumped off the stool. Onto his foot. He swore and nearly smacked Dace with his drink.

"Just don't agree to do anything with Dace and Clay and the boys," I cautioned. "At least not around that rocket fuel you call booze cooling the plumbing." And slunk back into the festivities.

What I didn't realize at the time, but should have, was that numerous fluid ounces of Purple Jesus had already cooled *his* plumbing, and would continue to for the next thirty-six hours. I therefore don't know why I was surprised when, somewhere between a few cuts off a live Mason Ruffner album and a stone-evil set of Stevie Ray Vaughn, he got a familiar glint in his eye, grabbed Dace and Clay, and hustled me into the kitchen with them.

"Grab your stuff," he chortled. "We're going to Brunswick."

"As in . . . uh . . . New Jersey?" I offered.

He shook his head. "Georgia, actually . . . "

I studied him fairly dispassionately for about ten seconds, then cracked.

"Oooo-ooohhhh, no-oo-ooo," I softly wailed, "you don't want to do this . . . not Brunswick, Georgia . . . not at 2 A.M. . . . not on several quarts of grain alcohol and fruit juice . . . not while fifty bar-buddies and their plush female friends are passing out onto your throw cushions and retching on the dog up here in New York . . . *No-oo-oooo . . . "*

His smile was not so much a grin as it was an atavistic baring of the teeth. I sighed. "What's Delta's next flight out?"

He grinned even wider. "It's no big deal," he explained. "We're just going to move a house."

I examined the toe of my boot with deep and sudden interest. "I see," I acknowledged, somewhat crisply. "*Just like that.*"

"No," he said, "we've gotta float it uprivvuh, fuhhst."

Of course.

There were a few other things that he forgot to mention. Like how Dace got involved in moving a house in the first place. Like why it had to be floated upstream to Daufuskie Island, off Savannah. And like how what was described to me as merely "a house," in fact turned out to be a three-story Victorian mansion on St. Simon's Island, where we now stood—a hundred and ten miles downriver.

"You know Dace's brothuh is a restoration architect," my Southern Man told me. "Well, it seems this ol' house is th' last of its kahhnd built in the Sea Ah-lands—it's from the 1880s . . . early 1900s? Sumthin' lahhk that. In any case, a developpuh bought the prop-puhty it stands on an' offuhhed to sell it for one dollar to anyone willing to move it an' save it from demolition."

He mopped the sweat out of his eyes and mashed his hair back under his baseball cap. "So this heah South Carolahhna company—International Paper Realty—had just the place for it up in Daufuskie, an' that's whah we're movin' it." He flashed Dace a quick smirk, and playfully thumped my shoulders. "Dace's bro-thuh's wife's broth-huh owns a barge company in South Caro-lahhna. That brothuh has another brothuh who's a house mover.

Dace ain't been down to this neck of th' woods in a little whahhl, so when his brothuh Bill—the architect—tol' him about the house, Dace said he'd come down an' help his sistuh-in-law's brothuhs with this little project."

"It's fam'ly," Dace said simply.

"An' history," said his buddy.

"An' them Oswolt brothuhs sure pay well," Dace added.

I stared both men into ash on a single heat-filled look.

"If I wasn't on vacation anyway, I'd kill both of you in your sleep for this." I pulled my hair up into a cap, jammed my sunglasses on, and seethed. "Although, not *many* get people to spend their vacations on a chain gang in the Deep South." The sarcasm was lost on both of them.

"Good sport, that woman," said Dace.

"Fawh' a Yankee," his buddy acknowledged.

Moving a house is not particularly hard. Moving three hundred tons of history is, especially when the house in question is the size of two football fields. Fortunately, though, Sea Island houses are usually built on pilings, and once you get an ex-Coast Guard crew chief, twenty-odd movers, and fifteen bargemen to rip off the latticework, thread thirty tons of steel beams under the crawl space, wheel a few hydraulic jacks under the structure, and jack the whole thing up *while keeping it level*—well, hey, the rest is easy. Really. You then have another ten days to winch the house onto sixteen wheels running on a two-train system and ease it on down a causeway that your trusty work crew just happened to bulldoze—when they weren't painstakingly peeling trellises off the mansion, or hauling beams in temperatures pushing 117° in the shade, or watching an architectural behemoth swing, ever so slightly, in the gluey air while a sweaty, swearing knot of men arm-wrestle it onto the conveyor. And *then* down to the water—because trucking it would have meant rolling the whole thing down the width of three interstate highway lanes.

I try not to think about those ten days. Because at the end of that time, with three blue whales' worth of beached house, we sat on one of the two barges they had grounded and lashed together and waited for high tide. And waited. And waited.

He managed a frail, sheepish half-grin. "An' Ah bet you thought this was gonna be all pure fun."

I controlled an overpowering urge to winch the house onto *him*. "If you even speak to me before we reach Savannah," I hissed, "I will personally have you towed, face-down, all the way to Daufuskie."

He considered that scenario fleetingly. "Ah guess I'd best take you ovvuh to Hilton Head for a few days' R-an'-R aftuh this."

"I guess so," I told him. "And I guess it better involve peace, quiet, a pool, air-conditioning, and a real menu—just so you know what to look for."

He rolled anthracite eyes at Dace and whistled tunelessly through his teeth. "Right. Any resort with a peach-colored restaurant that knows what an artichoke is."

I smiled tightly, thin-lipped as a razor cut. "Pretty much," I hissed. The two of them just moped.

It took two days to make the Great Float itself, and another two days for the tide to ebb so that the mansion could be off-loaded. By day two, we were all sunburned, sweaty, and exhausted; by day three, we were all sweaty, sunburned, exhausted, and bored; and by day four, crazed by dehydration and visions of the *New York Times*, a cool bath, and a four-line phone dancing in my head, I seriously contemplated desertion. Mine. And murder. His.

He, naturally, couldn't have cared less. This is where the Idle Mischief element enters the picture. Southern Men are naturally gifted storytellers. They claim they come by it honestly, from an oral tradition passed down through the generations. They also claim that this isn't lying, per se, but "dissembling." I claim that no matter where they come from, a group of bored, intelligent men packed together *will* drift on over to where the food, coffee, or booze is and proceed to lie through their teeth about any topic they happen to get ahold of. And they will *keep on* lying until laryngitis, incredulity, or a natural disaster in the form of an irate female comes along and stops them in their tracks. Or until the tide finally ebbs.

It was a miserable clump of haggard, peeling, hollow-eyed wraiths that straggled into the Hilton Head area that weekend. And it was an equally haggard host of revelers who greeted us at the door, four days later, when we finally made it back to New York—only to find the remains of the once-magnificent blow-out still going on. Oh, sure, at least half of the celebrants were more or less inert, and a few had actually gone to work or home in the last two weeks; but the survivors had had their number augmented by fresh arrivals of party-goers—and grain alcohol.

Clay had one eye glued shut from exhaustion, the other blood-shot beyond functioning. He grinned like an open wound. "We made a few more trips in your honor," he explained.

My Southern Male just buried his face in his hands and cackled. Then he and Dace took about three steps, pirouetted, and crashed to the floor in a brain-scorched coma. I dragged them by their heels into the bedroom and shut the door on the pair of them.

It was Dace's girlfriend who finally dared to approach me. "How can you stand that?" she demanded. "You knock yourself out fawh' them on your vacation, an' awhhl they do is come home an' pass out lahhk winos. How can you put up with that? Couldn't you get them to *do* anything?"

I took Jenny by the hand and led her through the clots of men still standing, through the dissemblers in the corner, the arm-wrestlers in the hall, the drinkers still hanging off the bar, and finally, to the two mansion-movers sprawled in blissful, air-conditioned unconsciousness.

"Take a good look at this, girl," I said, "and tell me just what you would have them *do*."

The sound of breaking glasses and Purple Jesus-fueled pandemonium in top gear filtered under the door. A slow smile spread across her face as she sighed and shook her head. "Not a dahhmm thing," she chuckled. "Not a single dahhmn thing. Considerin' what they just put you through, Ah guess Ah shouldn't even suggest to Dace that the kitchen needs to be redone. He mahht actually do it."

"Think of it this way," I pointed out, "at least they're quiet, immobile, and incapable of mayhem. And they don't even have to be fed."

Unlike the rocket-fueled frolickers we then clawed our way through . . . in the booze and the broken glass. Always let sleeping dogs lie. So to speak.

20 Cahhyit-fish Is Jumpin', and Business Is Boomin'

My first mistake was to let him read. At all. Under the heading Agriculture, the magazine he held carried an article about some enterprising Southerners expanding into aquaculture—fish-farming, to be precise. And the fish they were farming was—what else?—catfish.

Let me make a few things perfectly clear: first of all, I genuinely like fish. I like them in water, in fish tanks, and, occasionally, on my plate. I genuinely like catfish, too. Like tapirs, Shar-Pei puppies, and a few other animals I've met, they're just grotesque enough to be adorable. You can't help but feel a certain amount of affection for something so seriously ugly, mainly because few other people will. But I was a little sensitive on the subject of fish, in relation to him, because I knew full well that what would begin as a casual interest would develop into a full-fledged obsession; and before you could say high tide, we'd be knee-deep in catfish, bewildered Yankees, and a horde of beer-guzzling, slime-covered, bait-scrounging fishing buddies, cheerfully reeking camaraderie, brine, and debauchery all over the house. Oh, goody, goody.

I was also a little sensitive about his entrepreneurial instincts. *He* may have forgotten about the great computer fiasco of 1984, but I hadn't. Nor had I forgotten about that little arrangement with the private planes, the ten points of that off-Broadway show he had bought into, or a slew of other debacles too convoluted to describe. Please, God, not *catfish! Not in New York!* At least he and his business partner could lug the computers around without getting run out of town or manhandled by a seethe of hostile East Side doormen; I wasn't sure, however, that their tolerance would extend to catfish. Alive or iced. As a business venture, then, catfish were pisces non grata in my book. I just had to dissuade *him.*

He rolled forlorn brown eyes at me. "Y'cay-yant fish cahhyit-fish in these wawhtuhs," he mourned.

"I know," I said, "that's why they're breeding them down there, and shipping them across the States."

"It's no fun that way," he explained. "They taste better self-caught." I made sympathetic noises at him. He was unconvinced. "But we *need* cahhyit-fish in New Yawwhk!" Now *I* was unconvinced. He got one of my best flat, thousand-yard stares for his trouble.

"Don't you care about cahhyit-fish?" he burst out.

I pondered that for several seconds.

"No," I concluded.

His face hardened into a tight, unsmiling mask. He drummed his fingers on his thighs for a minute, then phoned his best friend.

"Clay!" he barked, "She don't care about cahhyit-fish!" I heard several loud, horrible gagging noises coming down the line. Obviously Clay was a little put out. "Yeah, that's how Ah felt," my Southern Male assured him. "Maybe if she ate one, she'd feel differently." More rapid-fire, staccato noises from the other end. He replaced the receiver, and bathed me in a neon grin.

"Girl," he informed me, "you're gonna meet some genuine Suth-uhhn cahhyit-fish!"

Let me make something else perfectly clear: *both* of these two connoisseurs of catfish were from Virginia. Richmond, Virginia. A real city—and a state capital to boot. It wasn't like they were bred up from the mud of the Mississippi Delta, or kidnapped at birth by Cajun terrorists and force-fed the bounty of the bayous—not by a long stretch. But one of the most interesting things about Southerners is that, regardless of where they were raised, all Southern food, all regional customs and traits, become theirs. The ones they like, that is. But catfish was a little tricky. They knew they liked it; they just didn't know *why*.

I maintained it was pure elitism on their part, not the lure of profit. Just as some of the limousine liberals of Yankeeland undergo sporadic fits of compassion for the city's underprivileged, transplanted Southerners demonstrate their authenticity by trying to out-Dixie the rankest, hardtackiest, most aboriginal cracker ever to crawl into daylight from the scrubby pine barrens or mudflats or stump-warted bogs of Sump Hell, U.S.A. Out of the primordial slime.

That's why I understood catfish just fine. Whether you liked it or not as food, it was wonderful as a living icon of Southern culture. There are, no doubt, Southerners who would opt faster for Nova Scotia salmon in a subtle little dill sauce; there are also, I am sure, Southerners who have never met a catfish, face to face, either at the end of a hook, or as dinner; but there are still a few Southerners left, who, given the chance, would string a whole chain of Bayou Bob's Catfish Cornucopia—or something like it— across an unsuspecting America. I know. I heard Clay suggest it.

"Figures," he said. "If Paul Prudhomme can grill up blackened redfish an' get these fool Yankees to eat it at thirty dollars a shot, whah cay-yant we make cahhyit-fish trendy?"

My Southern soulmate thought about that. "Whah not?" he replied. "'Cept we're gonna have to come up with a few ways to sneak it past 'em—at least until we get 'em sold on it."

"Lookit," said Clay, "we fry 'em. Stick 'em on buns. Grill 'em.

Make fish fingers out of 'em. Stew the dahhm things until the flesh falls off th'bone—hell, I don't know! Think lahhk a Yankee, for a minute—what would *you* do to a dead cahhyit-fish?"

His erstwhile business partner stared at the one on his plate. "Well, Ah'd make sure they'd removed the whiskers, foah' a start. . . . "

Clay drilled bullet holes through him with murderous eyes. "A-sahhd from decorating it!"

His buddy locked eyes with his dinner. "Ohhhh, Ah don't know . . . " he mused, "but Ah truly think you'd *have* t'disguise it, fuhsst." He looked up from his plate, grinning like a gargoyle. "This is New Yawwhk. Everywhere else in th'world, food is food. You eat it. Here, it's theater. You play with it. Man cay-yan't even get a hamburg-uh without some high-strung Food Artiste in sprayed-awhnn jeans throwin' parsley sprigs or aRU-gullah or something called 'radicchio' all over it. Dahhmm."

I fought back the urge to impale him on my fork. "Right," I seethed, "and you boil up a rodent or two, cover it in gravy and call it Brunswick Stew. Neat stuff."

Clay smiled like a switchblade opening. "And just what is wrong with Brunswick Stew?" he inquired coolly.

I batted large, innocent eyes at him. "Why, nothing," I purred. "I just wish you'd skin the squirrels *first*."

Two pairs of furious eyes bored holes through the top of my head, but I wasn't having any of it.

"Nuh-*uhhh*," I warned, "not this time! No chance! You wanted to go into real estate, and instead, wound up spending $90,000 just gutting and re-doing *your* apartment—fine! I didn't say anything. I lived in stray wiring and loose plaster for six months. You two then pulled that fast one with Clay's trust fund, his Daddy's lawyers, and a once-perfectly respectable female bank officer—*fine*! I didn't say a word! You racked up $3,000 in flowers, dinners, balloon-o-grams and I don't know what else, to get some Murray Hill heiress to convince her family to invest in the electronics firm—and I didn't say a word. *Not one word*! But I'll tell you right now—don't you dare even think about shipping catfish to New York, and don't you dare try to tell me it'll wipe nouvelle 'designer food' off the map, because then you will NEVER HEAR THE END OF IT, GOT THAT?"

I fell back into my chair, and pressed my bulging temples back in place.

The two men exchanged uncertain glances. It was a while before either ventured to speak. Finally my Southern Man cleared his throat, scratched his chin, and warily met my eye.

"Uhhhh . . . hon?" he rasped.

"*What?*" I snapped. Clay winced and looked away.

"Just . . . what is so *wrong* about cahhyit-fish?"

I sighed. "I know what you're thinking. Really. New Yorkers are eating all kinds of off-beat fish. Monkfish. Greenlipped New Zealand mussels. Buffalo-fish. Mako sharks. Dogfish eels and sea robins, for God's sake—who the hell ever grew up eating *sea robins*? So, what's one more offbeat fish, right? Besides, catfish are fine-textured, neutral-tasting, and you can do just about anything with 'em and they'll taste just great. I know. But,"—I sucked in my breath and crossed my fingers—"they aren't buying catfish in Manhattan! Surprise! The market's over-saturated with fish! And six months from now, something *else* will be over-saturating the place—figged chicken wings! Pizza with lamb sausage! Who knows! And guess what? The scant amount of catfish they *do* use up here, they don't advertise! They use it in filet-o-fish or Whaler Whopper sandwiches in fast-food joints, and call it sole or cod or whitefish of some persuasion—what do those dumb Yankees know, anyway? And finally—guess what? How many *real* restaurants not only use catfish, but actually *call* it "catfish" on the menu? Lutèce? Hell, no! The Four Seasons? Dream on! I can tell you. Including every Southern hangout, every Creole joint and every Cajun place in the city—*two*, exactly. Cajun's, and the Gulf Coast, where we're sitting, right now. But—and this is the big 'but'—how many people do you see *actually ordering* fried catfish?"

Both men swiveled on their chairs, straining frantically to identify the various entrées. Shrimp rémoulade abounded. Crawfish étouffé, sure. Chicken grillade, tasso, blackened beef—sure. But it wasn't until they squinted off into the corner that they spotted the lone order of catfish, complete with a side order of hush puppies.

I think it was my Southern soulmate who found his voice first. "We-e-ell," he sighed, "Ah wasn't that fond of it, anyway."

Clay polished off his beer and shrugged. "Moah' fun catchin' them than marketin' them, too." He paused fractionally. "Even with awhhl the mud an' slahhm an' stuff." His fellow entrepreneur just moped.

* * *

Adventure, risk, and Thinking Big were, after all, some of the things that made America what it is today, so I don't suppose I should have been too surprised to hear the pair announce a few weeks later they'd found a new business. What I wasn't prepared for was the business itself.

"Alligat-uh skins," he told me.

I suppressed a high-octave scream, and dropped the phone instead.

"Are you there?"

"Yes," I croaked, "where are you?"

"In Louisiana," he said, "there's lots of gat-uhs down heah."

"I know," I shot back, "it's also illegal—in most parts of the States—to buy the skin without the gator *in* it." I rubbed my head and got a grip on my nerves. "How many have you bought?"

"Ah didn't," he declared.

Oh, no, I could just picture it. He was down there, thrashing around in the bayous, blasting alligators out of the swamps with a gaggle of wild-eyed trappers cackling happily and congratulating him in jagged Cajun French. Oh, God.

"How many have you poached, then?"

"Ah *didn't*," he repeated, somewhat touchily, "Ah *acquired* it. Look, it's a little complicated, but Ah just have the one skin, an' Ah'll be back in town bah Sunday."

It was only because I had to hear how he got hold of it that I stood by while he whipped open his flight bag a few days later, smirked, and showed me a small, flat package wrapped in brown paper.

"It's actually a cayman skin," he informed me, "that's why it's so small."

He grinned again, and started undoing the twine. "They're fast, they're mean, and they're foul little SOBs, so nobody was too sorry to see this one go. Besahhds, lahhk Ah said, Ah only gawwht this one skin. Since Clay and Ah decided to stay outta th'gat-uh business, we thought y'oughtta have our sole hide."

He pulled the last shred of wrapping off it, and thrust into my hands a minuscule, hand-sewn, genuine cayman leather bikini.

Much later on, I came to feel deeply touched by my one-of-a-kind work of art, but at the time all I could do was to stand there with those few skimpy scraps of reptile in my hand, and start to shriek.

He glanced quickly at Clay, and chewed his lip. "Guess we finally went too fawh, this tahhhm," he opined.

And shut the bedroom door on my screaming.

Acknowledgments

Writing a book is more of a collabora-
tive effort than one would think. I owe
thanks to a host of garrulous friends for
talking their heads off: George Gwin,
Ron Ellis, and Donna Penyak; and to
Malinda Kat and Les for indulging a de-
ranged Yankee. And especially to Ed
. . . just for being Ed.

I would also like to thank my mother for
the faith, and my father for the humor.
And for the words.